Leckie ✕ Leckie

Scotland's leading educational publishers

D1580957

CfE Higher
BUSINESS MANAGEMENT
GRADE A BOOSTER

CfE Higher BUSINESS MANAGEMENT *GRADE A BOOSTER*

Anne Ross

ISBN 9780007590872

Published by
Leckie & Leckie Ltd
An imprint of HarperCollins*Publishers*
Westerhill Road, Bishopbriggs, Glasgow, G64 2QT
T: 0844 576 8126   F: 0844 576 8131
leckieandleckie@harpercollins.co.uk
www.leckieandleckie.co.uk

Commissioning editor: Katherine Wilkinson
Project manager: Craig Balfour and Keren McGill

Special thanks to
David Christie (copy edit)
Jill Laidlaw (proofread)
Louise Robb (proofread)
Lauren Reid (proofread)
Jouve (layout and illustration)
Ink Tank (cover)

Printed by CPI Group (UK) Ltd, Croydon, CR0 4YY

A CIP Catalogue record for this book is available from the British Library.

Acknowledgements
All images © Shutterstock.com
Questions taken from SQA past and specimen papers reproduced with permission, copyright © Scottish Qualifications Authority.

Whilst every effort has been made to trace the copyright holders, in cases where this has been unsuccessful, or if any have inadvertently been overlooked, the Publishers would gladly receive any information enabling them to rectify any error or omission at the first opportunity.

Contents

Introduction

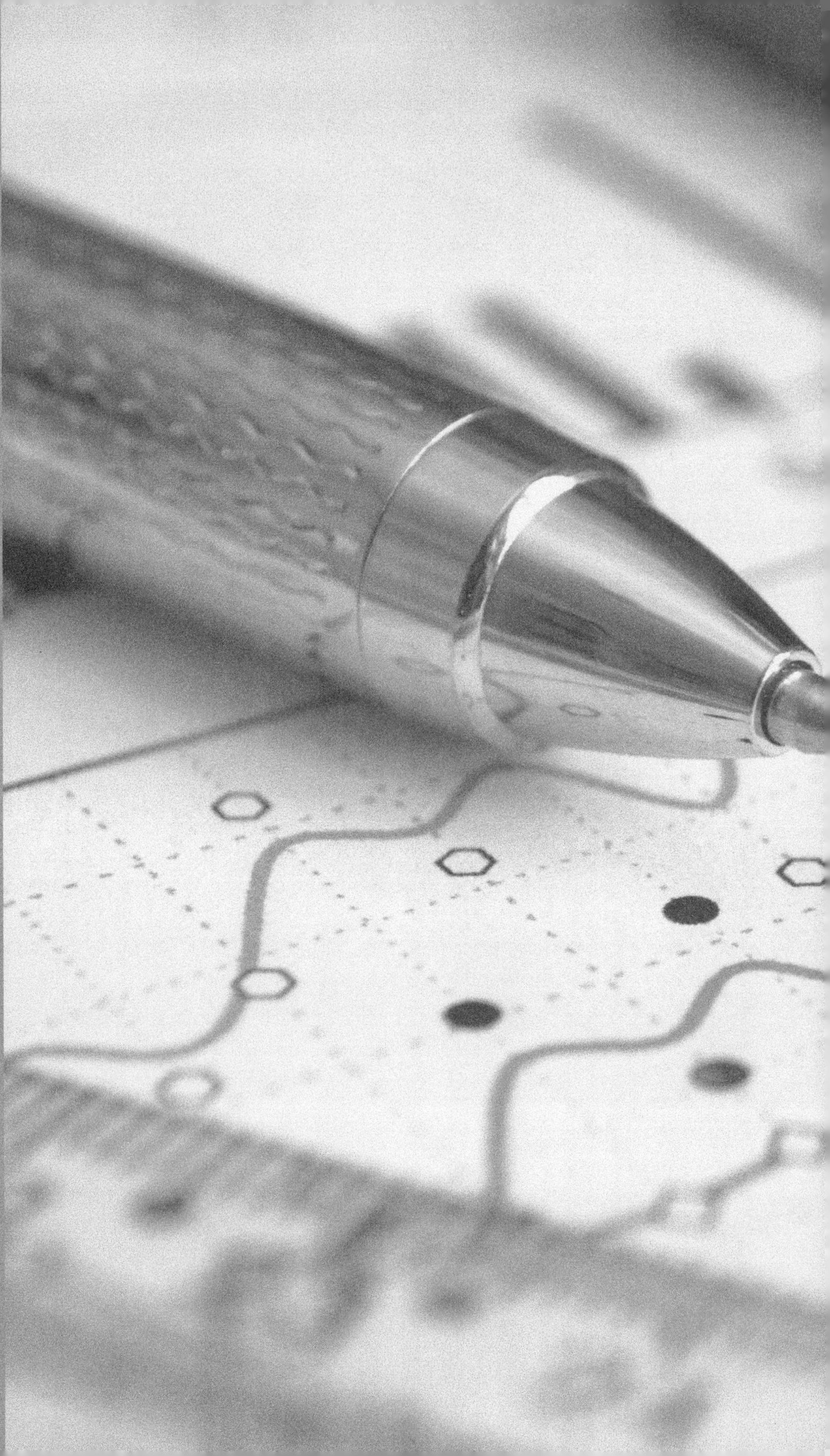

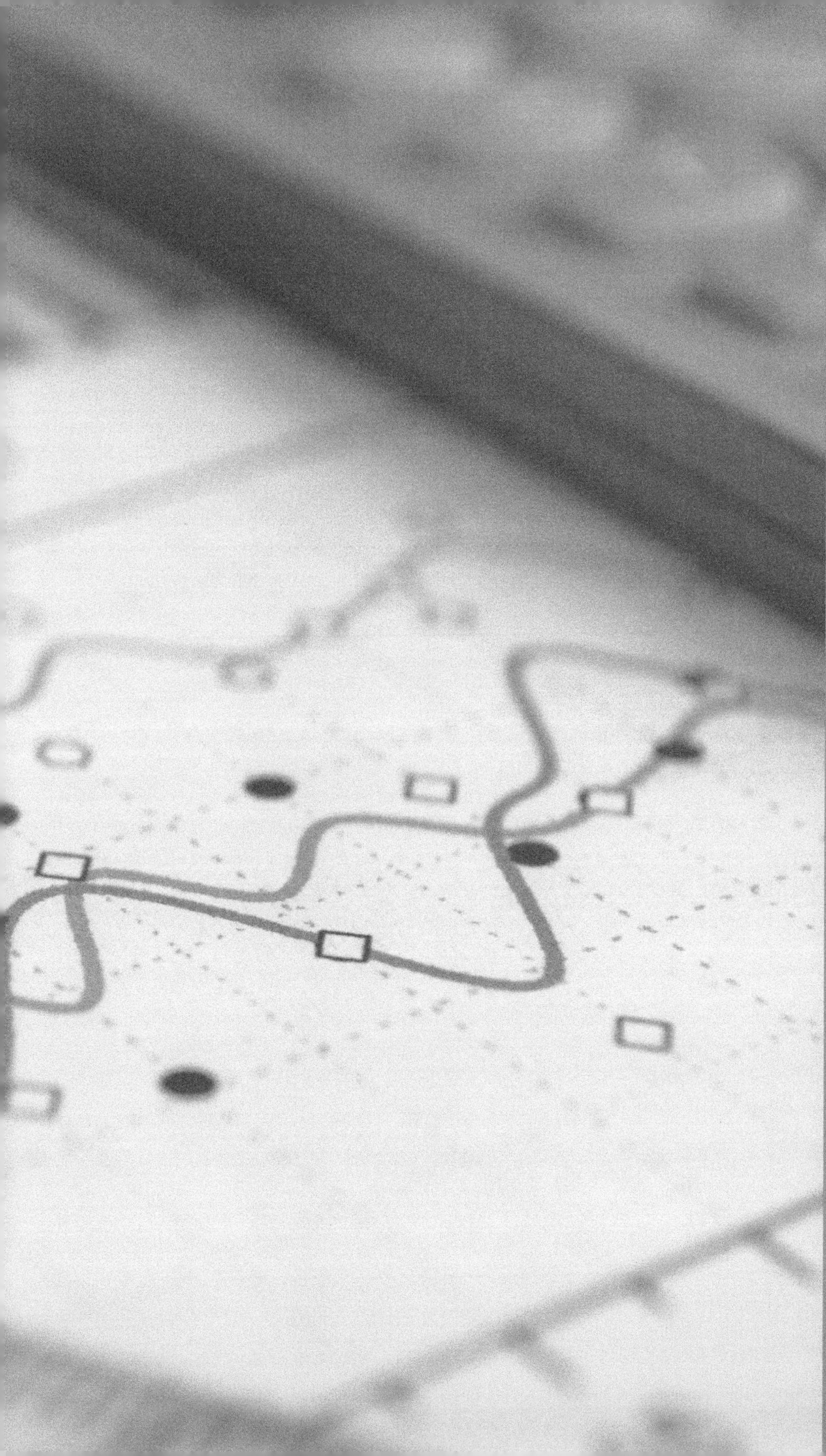

Introduction

Introduction

This book gives you advice on how to improve your grade in Higher Business Management. Business Management is an exciting and dynamic course that gives you insight into how businesses operate in our society. You will use a range of literacy and numeracy skills as well as problem solving abilities in order to navigate your way through the course. However, what you must be prepared to do more than anything else is read. The key phrase is 'reading for understanding'. Each time you read a piece of business information you must really ask yourself – what does this mean for business, and what are the consequences of this?

What is in this book?

This book gives you information about the course assessment. It outlines the requirements for unit assessments as well as the final examination. It gives you comprehensive information on how to prepare an assignment that will achieve a high score. This book gives you detailed information on how to cope with the command words of the final exam as well as giving you model answers. Many students do not score high marks in Business Management as their answers are too brief or vague or they simply give information about a topic instead of answering the specific question.

The course structure

There are three units in the course and they are studied by everyone. They are outlined in the table below:

Unit 1	Understanding business
Unit 2	Management of people and finance
Unit 3	Management of marketing and operations

Overview of unit assessments

Unit assessments are not graded; they are assessed on the basis of pass or fail. However, it is important from the outset to make the connection between what you learn in the unit assessments and how this relates to your answers in the final examination.

Unit 1: Understanding business

There are two learning outcomes in this unit. Each learning outcome has a number of assessment standards that you have to answer satisfactorily.

Outcome 1
Analyse the features, objectives and internal structures of large organisations by:

1.1 Comparing features of large organisations from different sectors of the economy.

1.2 Identifying the objectives of large organisations and describing the importance of these objectives.

1.3 Describing internal structures large organisations may use; justifying why they would use these structures.

Top tip

In this example, 1.1, 1.2 and 1.3 are the assessment standards. There are no marks allocated to these standards, which makes it difficult to know whether you have answered correctly or not. The general guidance is that if the assessment standard has a plural in the sentence you must give more than one, and to make sure you achieve a pass, you should aim for two or three correct answers.

Standard 1.1 above asks you to compare features of large organisations from different sectors of the economy.

- Features – more than one.
- Organisations – more than one.
- Different sectors – more than one.

Outcome 2

Analyse the environment in which large organisations operate by:

2.1 Explaining the impact of internal factors on a large organisation.

2.2 Explaining the impact of external factors on a large organisation.

2.3 Describing conflicts of interest that could exist between stakeholders.

Unit 2: Management of people and finance

There are two learning outcomes in this unit. Each learning outcome has a number of assessment standards that you have to answer satisfactorily.

Outcome 1

Apply knowledge and understanding of how the management of people can meet the objectives of large organisations by:

1.1 Describing approaches that could be used to manage human resources effectively.

1.2 Describing approaches that could be used to motivate staff to improve effectiveness.

1.3 Explaining how employee relations can impact on the success of a large organisation.

1.4 Describing the impact of current employment legislation.

Outcome 2

Analyse how the management of finance contributes to the effectiveness of large organisations by:

2.1 Describing sources of finance suitable for large organisations and giving reasons for their use.

2.2 Describing the purpose of financial (final accounting) statements.

2.3 Describing accounting ratios and outlining the use or limitation of ratio analysis.

Unit 3: Management of marketing and operations

There are two learning outcomes in this unit. Each learning outcome has a number of assessment standards that you have to answer satisfactorily.

Outcome 1

Apply knowledge and understanding of how the marketing function enhances the effectiveness of large organisations by:

1.1 Explaining how market research can be used to enhance the effectiveness of large organisations.

1.2 Explaining how the marketing mix can be used to enhance the effectiveness of large organisations.

1.3 Describing the costs and benefits to large organisations of having a product portfolio.

1.4 Describing how current technologies are used in the marketing function.

Outcome 2

Apply knowledge and understanding of how the operations function contributes to the success of large organisations by:

2.1 Describing the features and outlining the purposes of an inventory (stock) management control system.

2.2 Explaining methods that can be used to ensure customers receive quality products/services.

2.3 Explaining the costs and benefits of production methods used by large organisations.

2.4 Describing how current technologies are used in the operations function.

Important information about unit assessments

The way in which unit assessments are undertaken will vary from centre to centre as there is a high degree of flexibility built into unit assessments. Outlined below are some important assessment conditions with which you should be familiar:

- Unit assessments are open book – this means you may use resources to help you. However, some teachers prefer to give closed book assessments in order to help prepare you for the final examination. Make sure you are clear whether you are completing open or closed book assessments.
- You must be given sufficient time in which to complete the assessments.
- You must work independently.
- You must be clearly instructed that an assessment is taking place.
- You will be given some choice about the way in which you present your assessment (e.g. PowerPoint, written responses, multimedia, etc.).

You may be assessed using a unit-by-unit approach, a combined approach or a portfolio approach. The features of each of these approaches are explained in the table below:

Type of approach	Features of this approach	What this means for the candidate
Unit-by-unit approach	Each unit is assessed after it is completed and each outcome can be assessed individually. It is very easy to keep track of completed assessments.	You can revise each outcome as it is completed, which means it is more fresh in your mind. You will have a number of assessments spread over the whole year.
Combined approach	All three units of the course are assessed in a major piece of work. The assessment is usually based on a business scenario that requires a great deal of time and preparation.	You will probably not be assessed until nearer the end of your course. This means that you will be revising units towards the end of the course, which is an added advantage in preparing for the final exam.

(continued)

Type of approach	Features of this approach	What this means for the candidate
Portfolio approach	All three units of the course are assessed as they are being delivered and usually the assessments arise naturally during the course of learning and teaching. You will be advised which pieces of work should be retained for your portfolio.	You will be assessed as you progress throughout the course and this approach usually reduces the number of assessment events you will undertake during class time.

All of the unit assessments ask you to answer according to the assessment standards so make sure you are clear what these are for each unit.

Overview of the final examination

The final examination is known as the question paper and lasts for 2 hours and 15 minutes. There are 70 marks to be gained in the examination. There is no choice in the examination. There are two sections as follows:

| Section 1 | This is a case study or stimulus material about a UK business. There is a considerable amount of information about the business, which requires careful reading to assimilate all the information. This is followed by a set of questions worth 30 marks that can be from any part of the course. The questions should be answered in the context of the stimulus material.

The case study contains a mixture of written text and diagrams and numerical information – this could be in the form of financial statements such as a profit and loss account and a balance sheet. This takes time to read and understand during the exam. |
|---|---|
| Section 2 | This is worth 40 marks and is made up of four questions that can be drawn from any part of the course. Each question is worth 10 marks and will assess knowledge and understanding and how this is applied. |

The command words

You cannot have come this far in your Business Management course without already knowing what the command words are and how to go about answering each type of question. The command words are detailed below, and will be used throughout this book. Paying careful attention to the command word used in a question and making sure you answer accordingly is the key to achieving a top grade in your final examination. Command words are used in lots of different subjects – knowing which are the most common in Business Management is going to put you ahead.

Compare

What this means and how to answer using this word
You should use key words to show the similarities:

- *are both*
- *similarly*
- *as well as*
- *the same as*

You should use key words to show the differences:

- *on the other hand*
- *whereas*
- *but*
- *however*

Here is an example answer to the question 'compare desk and field research':

Desk and field research are both methods of market research that can be used to find out about the needs of customers. Desk research involves using books, journals, and internet websites whereas field research involves carrying out surveys to ask people their direct opinions. Desk research uses secondary information whereas field research uses primary information.

Here is a sample 'compare' question from the 2015 Higher question paper:

> **Q** **Compare** the use of random sampling and quota sampling when carrying out market research. **2 marks**

A good answer for this question would be:

Random sampling involves gathering market research information from any section of the population whereas quota sampling involves gathering market research information from a certain section of the population, for example, teenage males aged 15 to 19. With random sampling, everyone has the same chance of being selected whereas with quota sampling you will only be selected if you meet the criteria.

Describe

What this means and how to answer using this word

Descriptions are based on your knowledge and understanding. They do not usually require you to solve a problem. You are simply describing what you know and have already learned. You should write a factual account of what you are asked for. You can write about the features or uniqueness. You must write in sentences rather than bullet points or a list. The more information you can give the better. Describe is often used with other key words, for example:

- *Describe factors…*
- *Describe ways in which…*
- *Describe methods of…*
- *Describe how…*
- *Describe the best way of…*
- *Describe the features of…*

Here is a sample 'describe' question from the 2015 Higher question paper:

Q **Describe** the features of Maslow's motivation theory.   **5 marks**

A good answer for this question would be:

Maslow's motivation theory is based on a hierarchy of needs. Maslow classified these needs into different categories and claimed that employees would be motivated to have these needs met. Once they were met at the bottom level, they would move up to the next level. The needs can be seen in the diagram below:

Physiological needs include hunger and thirst. Safety needs include security and protection. Social needs means employees need to feel they belong to the business. Esteem needs include employees feeling they are achieving and getting on – then they will be motivated to achieve their highest potential, which is called self-actualization needs.

Discuss

What this means and how to answer using this word

Discuss is asking you to talk; it is almost like having a conversation with the examiner. During this conversation you are telling the examiner about the good and the bad, plus points and negative points, advantages and disadvantages, strengths and weaknesses, and arguments for and against. Remember, you must write in sentences and not just make a list of points. You may use similar words and phrases as for 'compare' questions.

Here is a sample 'discuss' question from the 2015 Higher question paper:

| Q | **Discuss** the effects of the Equality Act 2010 on an organisation. | **3 marks** |

A good answer for this question would be:

The effects of the Equality Act 2010 bring both advantages and disadvantages to any organisation.

The first advantage is that the organisation cannot be accused of any discrimination if they follow the law. Their employees' composition will include a range of ages, a good gender balance and different nationalities.

The second advantage is that employees who work for the organisation will be happy that everyone is treated equally and fairly. Therefore, the employees will be more motivated to work harder.

The first disadvantage is that the law is complex and requires all employees to be trained, especially those who work in Human Resources. This training costs time and money.

The second disadvantage is that the law may require the organisation to make physical adjustments to the building to make it accessible to all, for example, lifts, ramps for wheelchairs, etc. This also costs money.

Explain

What this means and how to answer using this word

Explaining is always the most difficult command word to master. Many candidates describe when they are supposed to be explaining; explanations are more complex and they do not involve descriptions. Explain means making it clear why something is the way it is or giving reasons why something has happened and the effects that it will have. To make your explanation clear you can back up what you have said with linking words, for example:

- *Therefore, it is clear that…*
- *This means that…*
- *The reason for this is…*

Here is a sample 'explain' question from the 2015 Higher question paper:

> Q **Explain** the benefits of positive employee relations. **3 marks**

A good answer for this question would be:

The first benefit of positive employee relations is that employees will feel motivated at work because they feel they are listened to and are valued. This means that their work rate and the quality of their work will improve.

The second benefit of positive employee relations is that this can be passed on to customers. Happy employees often relate this to customers. This means that customers will return to the business, therefore increasing sales and profit.

The third benefit of positive employee relations is that new customers can be attracted into the business. Existing customers will pass on the good reputation of the business. This means that the business could possibly increase their market share, sales and profit.

Justify

What this means and how to answer using this word
Justify asks you to give reasons for something. This is often used with suggest ('suggest and justify…').

Here is a sample 'justify' question from the 2014 Higher question paper:

> Q **Justify** the use of staff training for an organisation. **4 marks**

A good answer for this question would be:

The reasons why an organisation trains its staff are given below:

The first reason for training staff is that it is important for staff to learn and develop their skills because the more skilled the workforce, the better the quality of the finished product.

The second reason for staff training is that staff are often asked to cover for absent colleagues. Covering for colleagues means that staff need to know about the jobs these colleagues do.

The third reason **for training staff is to ensure that staff can follow health and safety guidelines. Staff need to know what the laws are and how they can follow the law** because **otherwise there may be accidents and injury.**

The fourth reason **for training staff is that it improves the image and reputation of the organisation. More high calibre workers can be attracted if they feel they will be offered training that will help them to improve their jobs.**

Overview of the assignment

The assignment is worth 30 marks and it is usually undertaken towards the end of the course. The assignment allows you to extend your knowledge and understanding and to apply this to a business of your choice to produce a report and come to researched conclusions. Your preparation and production of this assignment is extremely important as this gives you the opportunity to gain a potential 30 marks towards your final course award.

One of the most important points you have to take into account is that you have to use a business analytical tool to base your assignment on. There are a few well-known tools you can use, for example, SWOT analysis, PESTEC analysis and product portfolio analysis. What you should do is gather information as you study your course so that you have a clear idea of what you want to use when the time comes to prepare the assignment.

Top tip

Good assignments contain the following:

- Information on the chosen topic.
- Information on the chosen analytical tool.
- Background information on the business.
- Information about sources of information and what they were used for.
- Analytical and interpretative comments about the business topic.
- Diagrams, charts, graphs and pictures to illustrate important points.
- Conclusions and recommendations.
- Appendices.
- No more than 10 pages in total.

A full chapter is dedicated to the assignment later in this book.

Chapter 1: Understanding business

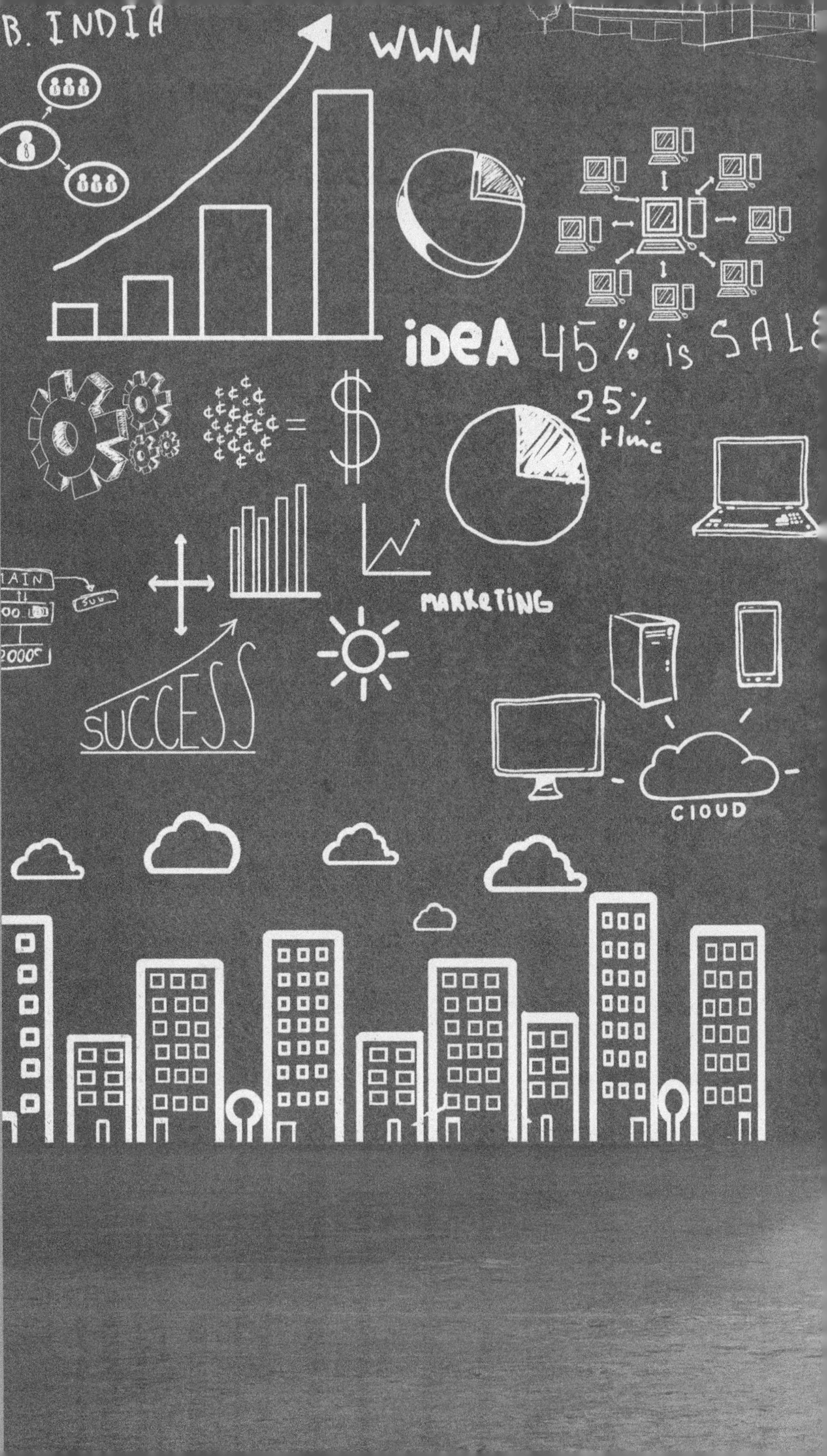

Understanding business

This is usually the first unit undertaken by students studying Higher Business Management. It sets the scene for how business is organised in our society and the environment in which businesses have to operate.

Outcome 1

Outcome 1 asks you to analyse the features, objectives and internal structures of large business organisations. This is broken down into three assessment standards.

Outcome 1.1

The first assessment standard asks you to compare the features of large business organisations from different sectors of the economy. Remember the key words you can use to compare – on the other hand, also, but, in addition.

The features of large organisations are ownership, control and finance. In other words, who owns the business, who runs the business or makes decisions and where the business gets its finance. However, different sectors of the economy include the public sector, the private sector and the third sector. The table below shows some of the comparisons you could make.

Type of business	Sector		Type of business	Sector
Private limited company	Private sector		Local council	Public sector
Public limited company	Private sector	Compare with	Social enterprise	Third sector
Charity	Third sector		Central government	Public sector

Sample answers include:
- *A public limited company (PLC) is owned by shareholders whereas the local council is owned by the taxpayer.*
- *A public limited company is controlled by a board of directors whereas the local council is controlled by councillors who are elected by the voters.*
- *A public limited company raises its finance from selling shares on the stock exchange whereas the local council raises its finance from council tax and grants from the government.*
- *A charity is not owned by anyone in particular and neither is central government.*
- *A charity is controlled by a board of trustees who run the charity for the benefit of the cause whereas central government is controlled by members of parliament who make decisions for the whole country.*
- *A charity raises its finance from donations and fundraising events whereas central government raises its finance from taxes, including income tax and corporation tax.*

Outcome 1.2

The second assessment standard asks you to **identify** the objectives of large business organisations and detail the importance of these objectives.

Identifying objectives is usually straightforward and includes:

Identifying objectives	Importance of these objectives
Profit maximisation	Businesses want to make as much profit as possible in order to be as successful as possible.
Social responsibility	Businesses want to be socially responsible in order to attract as many customers as possible and to gain a positive image in the community.
Sales revenue maximisation	Businesses want to ensure that they can obtain as much revenue as possible in order to cover their costs.

(continued)

Identifying objectives	Importance of these objectives
Growth	Businesses want to grow in order to become more successful and to compete with others.
Survival	Sometimes businesses just aim to survive and to keep trading when economic conditions are difficult.
Increase market share	Businesses want to increase their market share so that revenue/customers will increase and, therefore, their profits overall will increase.

Outcome 1.3

The third assessment standard asks you to describe the internal structures of large organisations and to justify why the business would use this structure.

Internal structures could include:

Structure	Description	Justification
Grouping of activities	This involves organising the business in terms of the particular activities carried out. For example, by function, by product, by customer and by location.	Functional grouping allows experts to carry out the specialist functions of *marketing, operations, human resources* and *finance*. This should lead to more efficiency as experts deal with the day-to-day work. Product grouping allows departments to specialise in that particular product, thus ensuring specialist product knowledge. Grouping by customer allows customers' needs to be met if they are organised by market segment. Grouping by location allows customers to have access to local offices and for their local needs to be met.

(continued)

Structure	Description	Justification
Tall structure	This is a hierarchical structure with many levels of management and a long chain of command. The span of control can be very narrow.	This allows instructions to be clearly passed down the chain of command. Everyone is very clear who his or her line manager is. There are multiple opportunities for promotion; this can motivate employees to improve their skills through additional training.
Flat structure	This is a structure with few levels of management and a short chain of command. The span of control can be very wide.	This is useful as communication is very quick and easy and everyone is well informed about decisions. Employees can work in teams, which improves their motivation.

There are other structures that you can describe, for example, matrix, centralised and de-centralised and entrepreneurial structures. The important point here is that you must **describe the structure and justify why the structure is used**.

Outcome 2

Outcome 2 asks you to analyse the environment in which large organisations operate. This is all about internal and external factors and stakeholders.

Outcome 2.1

The first assessment standard asks you to explain the impact of internal factors on a large organisation.

Internal factors are outlined on page 22. However, it is very important to understand that you are being asked about the **impact of internal factors** – not just a description of what they are.

Human resources

These are the employees of the organisation. Employees can affect the organisation by their work standards and effort or motivation. If employees are producing poor quality work, customers will not be happy and they will not return. This will also affect any potential new customers. If employees are not motivated they will not produce good results, customer service will be poor and the reputation of the organisation will suffer. If employees are not properly trained then this can also affect their performance. Overall sales and profits of the organisation or business can fall because of the performance of employees.

Positive factors arise from good employee performance. If employees are very skilled at their jobs and deal with customers correctly, then this will encourage customers to come to the business.

Finance

This is finance available for expansion, for example, buying new equipment, premises, etc. If there is a lack of finance for investment, the business or organisation will struggle to compete. Finance is needed for new machines, equipment, technology, repairs, etc. Without this investment, growth will not be possible and the organisation can stagnate.

When finance is available businesses are able to fulfill their objectives more quickly, for example by employing new staff or developing new products. At the higher end of the scale finance might be available for new premises or for research and development.

Technology

This is new technology that covers a range of ICT and production technologies, for example, computers, networks, mobile devices, robots, electronic assembly lines, etc. Organisations and businesses need to keep up to date with new technology. For example, global markets depend on the use of computer technology including laptops, tablets, smartphones, internet websites, etc. If the business does not access this technology, customers go elsewhere. Competition from other businesses is already strong in this whole area. Production technologies are moving ahead very quickly and businesses need to use new technology to survive.

When businesses are able to take advantage of new technology they are able to adopt new ways of working, which can give them a competitive edge and help them to attract new customers

Top tip

A word of advice on internal factors: it is still possible that the final exam could just ask you to describe the internal factors, so make sure you always <u>underline</u> the command word.

Outcome 2.2

The second assessment standard asks you to **explain** the impact of external factors on a large organisation.

External factors are outlined below. The same principle applies here. You are being asked about the **impact of external factors** – not just a description of what they are.

External factors are most easily remembered by PESTEC (political, economic, social, technology, environmental and competition).

Political

This is the influence of the government through laws businesses have to comply with. The impact of any laws passed is that the business has to follow them. This can mean that they have to spend more money to comply with the law, for example, health and safety laws involve training employees. Minimum wage laws mean that more is spent on staffing/wages so less is available to spend on other business expenses. Complying with laws can reduce profits but a positive impact of this factor is that businesses can be a safer place to work.

Economic

This is the influence of the economy on a business. It includes interest rates, the rate of unemployment and the influence of the stock exchange. If the economy is strong and interest rates are low, then this is generally good for business. Businesses can borrow money at low rates and there are customers to pay for their goods and services. In addition, if unemployment is low then people have money to spend. Obviously, the opposite is true when interest rates are high and unemployment is high. This is often referred to as booms and slumps in the economy. The impact is always the same – in a boom period, businesses benefit with higher sales and profits. In a slump, businesses often fail and employees lose their jobs.

Social

This is all about people – how they work and how tastes and fashions change. Working patterns have changed in the last 20 years and they will continue to evolve. The impact of this is that businesses have a wide range of employment options but also that employees can be difficult to recruit and retain. Businesses have to be more flexible in allowing working patterns to suit all types of employees, for example, parents, as well as those who are planning for retirement. Tastes and fashions also change and the impact of this is that businesses have to be able to adapt. For example, with an ageing population there will be more demand for products that assist old people such as mobility scooters.

Technology

This means using technology that will maximise customer contact and satisfaction with the business. The impact of technology means that businesses have to make sure they are using the most up-to-date technology to keep them competitive in the market. They must be able to contact their customers quickly and effectively using a range of ICT and mobile devices, for example, internet websites, smartphones, email, text messages, etc.

Environmental

This includes the weather but also factors such as recycling, reducing greenhouse gas emissions, etc. The impact of the weather on a business is usually noticed with extremes, for example, very hot or cold temperatures. A hot summer will have a positive impact on the sales of ice cream and summer clothes, which leads to increases in profit. A very cold winter will lead to an increase in demand for energy and warm clothes. In extreme cases, snow can prevent businesses from opening or customers getting there. All businesses need to think about recycling and reducing their carbon footprint. The impact of this is positive and negative. Positive in that it may attract more customers but negative in that it costs money to do these things.

Competition

This means other businesses who sell the same products and services. Competitors always have an impact on your business but again this can be positive or negative. Other businesses may be struggling with good quality goods and services, therefore, customers are attracted to your business. However, competitors may be lowering their prices or advertising special offers that pull

Top tip

A word of advice on external factors: it is still possible that the final exam could just ask you to describe the external factors, so make sure you always underline the command word.

your customers away. It is important to always know what your competitors are doing so you can change your business strategy in response.

Outcome 2.3

The third assessment standard asks you to **describe** the conflicting interest that could exist between stakeholders. There are two learning points you must already know about this:

1. Who are stakeholders?
2. What is the interest of each stakeholder?

Once you know these two important points, you should be able to describe possible conflicts between stakeholders. It is assumed that you already know the two points above so the responses below show potential conflicts between them. Some sample answers could be:

Employees want high wages whereas owners might not always be able to pay high wages if sales or profits are not high enough to justify this.

Employees want good working conditions, for example, more holidays and a welcoming environment, whereas owners might not be able to pay for these things if sales or profits are not high enough.

Managers want employees to work hard as the manager may receive a bonus based on this; however, employees may not be motivated by the manager, therefore, they do not perform to their highest standards.

Customers want good quality products and services at low prices; however, the owners may not be able to charge lower prices without the risk of failure.

Owners want suppliers to deliver good quality raw materials at low prices whereas suppliers need to be able to charge high prices in order to survive.

Local communities want to live in a peaceful environment without litter and pollution and can often demonstrate or complain about a business that pollutes. This gives the business owner a problem if he/she wants to continue to operate their business in the location.

Interdependence of stakeholders

Although the unit assessment does not directly ask you to do this, it is important that you understand the concept of stakeholder interdependence. Stakeholders depend on each other, even though they may be in conflict. For example, the manager depends on the employees to produce the goods and services. Customers depend on the business to provide them with their goods and services. The local community depends on the business to provide jobs for the area.

This is the end of the section on internal unit assessments for understanding business. Remember that everything you have learned for these unit assessments is valid and helpful for the final question paper.

However, it is also important to remember that the understanding business unit has a number of other topics that are not examined in the unit assessments.

Chapter 2: Management of people and finance

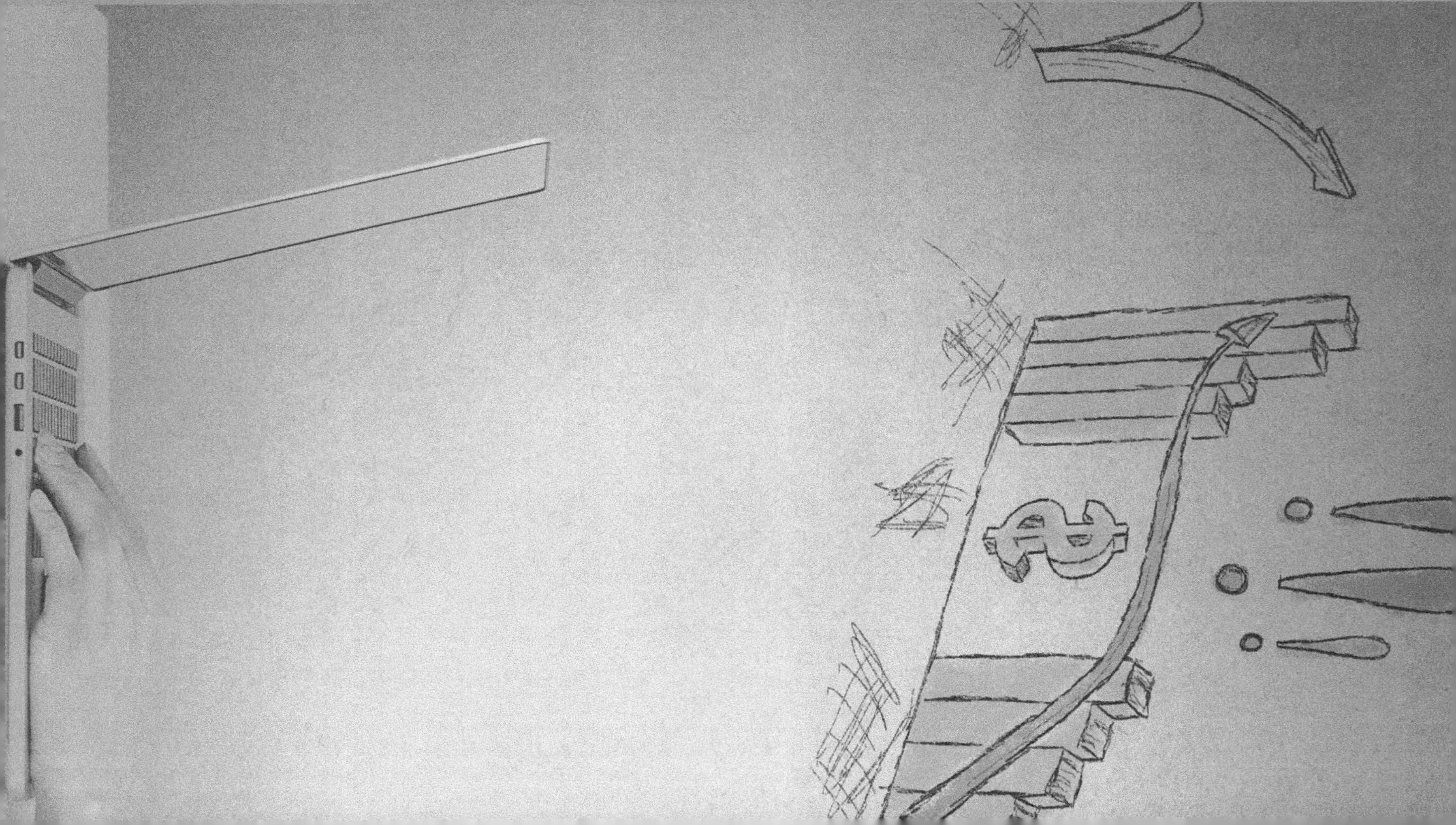

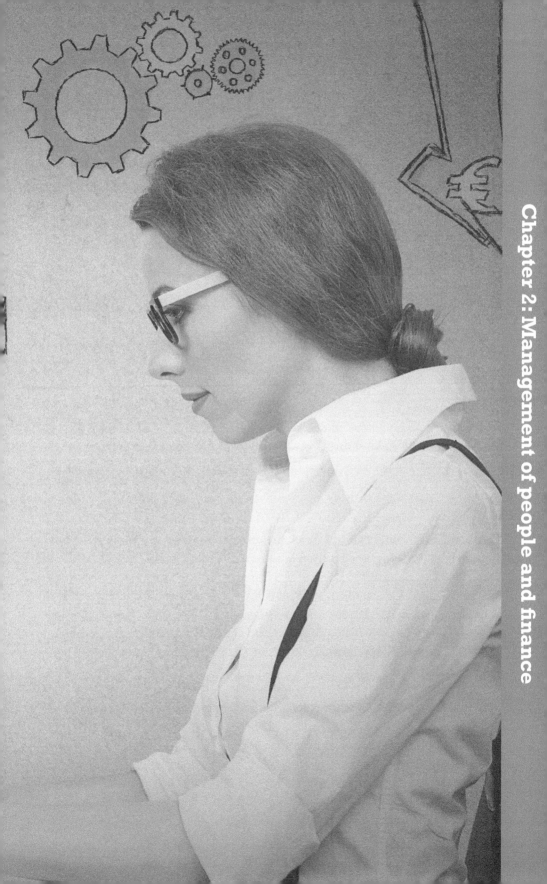

Management of people and finance

Outcome 1 of this unit asks you to apply your knowledge and understanding of how the management of people can meet the objectives of large organisations. This is broken down into four assessment standards.

Outcome 1

Outcome 1.1

The first assessment standard asks you to **describe** approaches that could be used to manage human resources effectively. This is a very straightforward outcome, as you only have to describe. Describing an approach just means how the business goes about doing this.

The most common approaches to managing human resources are described below.

Workforce planning

This is usually undertaken by senior management to try to achieve their strategic objectives. They plan in advance – how many employees do we need? What particular skills do they need? How long will we need these employees for? However, they also need to know if there are employees available and this involves analysing the labour market to see what is available. This could mean employers set up links with colleges and universities to try to encourage students to come and work for them when they have finished their course.

Recruitment

This involves people applying for jobs with the business. Recruitment has several identifiable steps, for example, identifying the job vacancy, conducting a job analysis, preparing a job description that outlines the duties and responsibilities of the job, preparing a person specification that outlines the skills and qualities required for the job and then advertising the job either internally or externally. The business might then send out application forms or ask for CVs to be sent in or they might open up an online application process on their website.

The recruitment process stops here. Some businesses and organisations use a recruitment agency to help them with this process.

Selection

The selection process begins once all the applications and CVs have been received. The process of selection involves narrowing down the applicants according to the person specification by matching them with the essential and desirable criteria. Thereafter, a shortlist is prepared and candidates can be invited for an interview where they will be asked questions or another selection method is used, for example, role play, giving a presentation, a team building task, etc.

Some businesses and organisations use assessment centres to carry out this part of the process. The assessment centre uses trained human resources specialists to do this.

Training

Training of employees is important in order to get the best from their performance. Training can be undertaken on the job or off the job. 'On the job' training involves training employees in the workplace through demonstration, coaching, job rotation, etc. It can be targeted specifically to the employee's needs. 'Off the job' training involves training away from the workplace and usually involves going to college or university. It can involve additional qualifications.

Outcome 1.2

The second assessment standard asks you to describe approaches that could be used to motivate staff to improve effectiveness. This is slightly more complicated as you have to show how the approach improves effectiveness. In other words, you need more than a description. Therefore, a good answer will follow the structure on page 32.

Top tip

Note the amount of detail that has been included for the description of each human resource management approach. However, note that this was a 'description' question and not a 'discussion' question, which would require you to give the advantages and disadvantages of each approach.

Approach	Description	How this will improve effectiveness
Offer employees a good career structure for promotion.	This means having levels of management or assistant management or supervisors that employees know they can apply for in the future.	This will improve effectiveness as staff will be motivated to achieve a promotion, therefore they will complete their work to a higher standard.
Offering good pay and conditions	Good pay usually means paying more than other businesses, whether it is the minimum wage or a much higher salary. Good conditions means a working environment that is comfortable and welcoming, good holidays, flexible working, etc.	This will improve effectiveness because employees will feel valued by higher rates of pay and will want to do a good job. A good working environment reduces stress for employees, which usually means their work performance will improve and this can lead to a lower staff turnover.
Staff appraisals	Employees are appraised by their line manager and targets are set for improvements in performance or targets for promotion.	Appraisals improve effectiveness because employees are very clear about what they have to achieve. The outcome of an appraisal may involve setting targets for attendance or an improved work rate or they may focus on bonuses for good work performance.
Works councils	Setting up a works council that is made up of representatives of employees and managers in order to make decisions.	This will improve effectiveness because employees will have a forum where they are consulted and listened to and have somewhere they can give their opinions. This usually makes employees feel more valued and more motivated to improve their work performance.
Employees of the month and achievement awards	This involves giving out certificates, prizes, bonuses or praise to employees who have performed well.	This improves effectiveness because employees will be motivated to improve their performance if they feel they have something to gain. Most employees respond positively to achievement awards.

Outcome 1.3

The third assessment standard asks you to explain how employee relations can impact on the success of a large organisation. This is similar to outcome 1.2 but it has a slightly different focus. This outcome focuses on the success of the organisation as a whole. Therefore, it is about achieving the business objectives that may include increased sales and profits. **This is an explain question so reasons must be given.**

Some sample answers could be:

Employee relations involves the communication that takes place between management and their employees. This takes many different forms and is linked to staff motivation because employees will feel more involved and likely to increase their work performance if they feel they have been listened to and have a role to play in decision-making. Therefore, consulting employees about any changes can increase work performance and possibly the sales and profits of the business.

Good employee relations can help to reduce staff turnover, as staff will be happy to work in a business that listens to them. This will reduce the need to recruit more employees, thus saving costs. A reduction in staff turnover will also reduce the need to train new staff. All this means that profits can rise.

Employee relations can help to reduce any possible industrial action. If employees and management have good communication, this will have a positive outcome with less chance of strikes or other disputes. This will enhance the reputation of the business overall.

Outcome 1.4

The fourth assessment standard asks you to describe the impact of current employment legislation. However, it is more specific than that. You have to identity one piece of current legislation and describe two effects of this law on either the employee or the organisation.

The laws that you can choose from are:

- Equality Act 2010
- Minimum Wage Act 1998
- Health and Safety at Work Act 1974

Some sample answers could be:

One law that impacts on a business is the Equality Act 2010. This means that employees cannot be discriminated against on the grounds of sex, religion, disability, race, pregnancy, etc. This means that all employees have equal rights.

The organisation must take into account this law when preparing job advertisements and job and person specifications. They must also consider this law when selecting candidates for an interview. If employees or candidates feel that they have been unfairly treated they can take the organisation to court.

The organisation may also have to pay for adjustments to the building or premises to ensure that employees or candidates with disabilities can access the workplace.

Another law that impacts on a business is the Minimum Wage Act 1998. This law sets the minimum wage that must be paid to employees according to their age. This means that employees are guaranteed a wage that will help them to plan their living expenses. The impact on the business is that they have to pay the wage regardless of the level of profits they are making. If the wage rate is increased by the government, the business has to pay more. This can reduce their profits.

Another law that impacts on a business is the Health and Safety at Work Act 1974. This law outlines the responsibilities of both employers and employees. The impact of this law on employees is that they must be trained in health and safety procedures and they must wear any protective clothing that is provided for them. The impact on the business is that they must pay for health and safety training and equipment as well as producing a health and safety policy statement that all employees must be able to access.

Outcome 2

Outcome 2 of this unit asks you to analyse how the management of finance contributes to the effectiveness of large organisations. This is broken down into three assessment standards.

Outcome 2.1

The first assessment standard in this outcome asks you to describe sources of finance suitable for large organisations and **give reasons for their use**.

Some sample answers are outlined below:

Bank loan

An amount of money borrowed from the bank and repaid over an agreed period with interest. Bank loans can be used for a number of reasons. For example, purchasing new equipment or machinery and spreading the cost over a specific period, paying to develop a new product or receiving a large sum of money up front if required to cover a period when cash is low.

Mortgage

An amount of money borrowed over a much longer period than a normal bank loan and paid back with interest, which is usually at a lower rate of interest than other bank loans. Mortgages are mainly used to purchase buildings or premises. Most business do not have access to the large sums of money needed for these purchases without the use of a mortgage.

Leasing

This involves obtaining assets, such as machinery and equipment, without buying them. The asset is 'rented' for a long period of time. The main reason for leasing assets is to avoid having to pay large sums of money that the business may not have. Leasing also allows machines and equipment to be obtained quickly.

Debentures

This is used by PLCs to raise finance. It involves asking members of the public to give a loan to the company, usually for a specific purpose. For example, many football clubs sell seats to fans as 'debentures'. The main reason for using debentures is that the money from the loans is kept by the business for a long time. In addition, debentures usually pay a fixed rate of interest; therefore, it is easier to plan financially.

Issue of shares

This is used by PLCs to raise finance. They can issue new shares at any time in the future within agreed limits. *The main reason for issuing new shares is that it is fairly easy and straightforward. The money is available quickly and many existing shareholders will take up new shares if they are happy with the performance of the company.*

Outcome 2.2

The second assessment standard in this outcome asks you to describe the purpose of financial (final accounting) statements.

This is fairly straightforward with only three statements that can be described here:

- The Trading Account
- The Profit and Loss Account
- The Balance Sheet

Some sample answers are:

The purpose of the Trading Account is to work out the profit made from buying and selling stock. This is known as Gross Profit.

The purpose of the Profit and Loss account is to work out the Net Profit, which is the profit made after buying and selling and all expenses have been deducted.

The purpose of the Balance Sheet is to show the total value of assets and liabilities of the business at a certain point in time. It shows the Net Worth of the business.

Outcome 2.3

The third assessment standard asks you to **describe** accounting ratios and outline their use or outline the limitations of ratio analysis.

You must be very careful to read the question carefully here as you can answer about *either* the uses of ratio analysis or the limitations of ratio analysis. The categories of ratios are profitability, liquidity and efficiency. The most common ratios are described in the table below with formulas shown for calculation:

Ratio	Description	Formula
Gross profit % (Profitability)	Shows how profitable the business is when buying and selling stock.	$\dfrac{\text{Gross profit}}{\text{Sales}} \times 100\%$
Net profit % (Profitability)	Shows how profitable the business is after all expenses have been deducted.	$\dfrac{\text{Net profit}}{\text{Sales}} \times 100\%$
Rate of stock turnover (Efficiency)	This shows how quickly stock is bought and sold during the course of the year.	$\dfrac{\text{Cost of goods sold}}{\text{Average stock}}$ The answer is expressed as times per year
Return on capital employed (Profitability)	This shows how much return the owners receive on the capital they have invested in the business.	$\dfrac{\text{Net profit}}{\text{Capital employed}} \times 100\%$
Current ratio (Liquidity)	This is the ratio of current assets to current liabilities and it shows how liquid the business is in terms of paying its short-term debts quickly.	Current assets : Current liabilities The answer is expressed as a ratio

The uses and limitations of ratio analysis are explained in the sample answers below:

Uses of ratio analysis

- *Ratios can be used to compare the performance of the business from one year to another.*
- *It is most useful when trends can be identified over a few years.*
- *Ratios can also be used to compare the performance of the business with other businesses in the same line.*
- *It is important to ensure that the comparison is like for like.*
- *When ratios differ from industry averages, the causes of these should be investigated by the business.*

Limitations of ratio analysis

- *Ratios do not always tell the full story, for example, there may be internal or external factors that have affected the business performance. For example, the business may have suffered from industrial action that has subsequently been resolved; there may have been staff absence or illness that affected performance.*
- *The ratios may vary from one year to another because of fluctuations in the economy.*
- *Comparing with other businesses is not always straightforward as other businesses may be bigger or smaller, even though they sell similar products or services.*

This is the end of the section on internal unit assessments for managing people and finance. Remember that everything you have learned for these unit assessments is valid and helpful for the final question paper.

However, it is also important to remember that the managing people and finance unit has a number of other topics that are not examined in the unit assessments.

Chapter 3: Management of marketing and operations

Innovation
Branding
Solution
Marketing
Analysis
Ideas
Success
Management

Business Str

Chapter 3: Management of marketing and operations

Management of marketing and operations

Outcome 1

Outcome 1 of this unit asks you to apply your knowledge and understanding of how the marketing function enhances the effectiveness of large organisations. This is broken down into four assessment standards.

Outcome 1.1

Outcome 1.1 asks you to *explain* how market research can be used to enhance the effectiveness of large organisations. The emphasis in your answer is on how market research improves effectiveness. This is **not** a description of market research.

Some sample answers could be:

- *Market research improves effectiveness because customers are asked their opinions about goods and services and if the business considers these opinions, they will be successful in selling these goods and services.*
- *Market research improves effectiveness because customers can be asked to test prototypes and give feedback. Once this feedback is considered, the business can be sure they have met customer needs.*
- *Market research improves effectiveness because asking customers for feedback ensures that the correct market segments are targeted for advertising and promotions, which saves wasting money on adverts that nobody will watch.*

Outcome 1.2

Outcome 1.2 asks you to *explain* how the marketing mix can be used to enhance the effectiveness of large organisations. This means explaining how the marketing mix can be altered to enhance effectiveness. Enhancing effectiveness in this context means increasing sales, profits, avoiding waste and increasing market share. You can explain any of the seven Ps of the marketing mix.

Some sample answers could be:

The price of the product can be altered – either increased or decreased. If the price is increased, this could attract some customers who think it is a high quality product and want to buy it. Increasing the price could also increase sales revenue provided the volume of sales does not fall. If the price is decreased, this could attract more customers and increase sales revenue. Overall altering the price can increase effectiveness provided it leads to an increase in sales revenue.

Altering the product itself can lead to increased sales. The product could be improved in some way, for example, changing the style, more colours offered, etc. Changes to the product may attract new customers and encourage existing customers to continue buying, which ensures greater customer loyalty. Either way, this could improve sales revenue and may increase market share, thus improving effectiveness overall.

Outcome 1.3

Outcome 1.3 asks you to describe the costs and benefits to large organisations of having a large product portfolio. Costs and benefits are also known as advantages and disadvantages.

> **Top tip**
>
> Note how much detail is put into these answers in order to meet the requirements of the command word 'explain'.

Advantages	Disadvantages
Having a large product portfolio can mean that the business can increase its profits as there are a variety of different products to sell to different target markets.	Having a large product portfolio can be very expensive to advertise and promote to ensure that every product gets the same coverage in the market.
Having a large product portfolio can mean that the business can launch new products easily and quickly as the business is already known to customers.	Having a large product portfolio can be a problem if one product fails or starts to go into decline. Customers can wrongly assume that a problem with one product means that there are problems with the whole portfolio.

Outcome 1.4

Outcome 1.4 asks you to describe how current technologies are used in the marketing function. Again, this is fairly straightforward as you are describing. **Be careful though, as the description is of how the technology is used and not a description of the technology itself.** Some sample answers are given below:

Technology	What this is used for
Internet website	A business can use an internet website to offer an online shopping experience for customers. Customers can sign up for an account and order and pay for products that will then be delivered either to their homes or to their nearest shop. The website can show pictures and prices of the products as well as other important information, for example, instructions and advice on how to look after the product.
Social media	A business can use social media, such as Facebook, to offer advice, information and special offers to customers. Customers can leave feedback and they can talk to other customers online about the products and services of the business. The business can also show pictures and prices of the products.

(continued)

Technology	What this is used for
Email	A business can use email to keep in touch with customers. Specific customers can be targeted with information about products and services they might be interested in or they can be invited to email their feedback or complaints.
Smartphones/ tablets	A business can develop an app for mobiles and tablets that allows customers to order goods and services through their mobile device and pay for delivery. An example of this is fast food such as Domino's pizza.

Outcome 2

Outcome 2 of this unit asks you to apply your knowledge and understanding of how the operations function contributes to the success of large organisations. This is broken down into four assessment standards.

Outcome 2.1

Outcome 2.1 asks you to describe the features and outline the purposes of an inventory (stock control) system. This also includes the benefits of a stock control system.

Features of a stock control system	Description
Maximum stock level	This is the most stock that should be held in the stock room at any time. It usually depends on the space available and the amount of stock that is used regularly.
Minimum stock level	This is the minimum amount of stock that should be held in the stock room at any time. It usually depends on the amount of stock that is used regularly and how long it takes to order and receive more stock.

(continued)

Features of a stock control system	Description
Re-order level	This is the level at which more stock is automatically re-ordered in order to avoid running out of stock. The re-order level is set higher than the minimum level.

Outline the purposes/benefits

One benefit of a stock control system is that the business is unlikely to run out of stock. Therefore, production orders can always be completed and customers will be happy.

One benefit of a stock control system is that the business is unlikely to over stock and run the risk of having too much stock, which can go out of date and become obsolete. This will cause them to lose money.

Outcome 2.2

Outcome 2.2 asks you to explain methods that can be used to ensure customers receive quality products/services. This time, the explanation involves giving a description and the benefits of the method.

Some sample answers are given below:

Quality method	Description	Benefits of this method
Quality circles	This is when groups of employees work together with management to develop quality approaches to their work. Employees' ideas can be taken into account.	Employees are given increased control over the production methods. Therefore, they are more motivated.
Quality control	This is when products are checked at the end of the production process to make sure there are no faults.	All products are checked at the end. Therefore, no faulty products should get through to customers.

(continued)

Quality method	Description	Benefits of this method
Quality assurance	This is when products are checked at every stage of the production process to make sure there are no faults.	Products are checked at each stage of the production process. Therefore, there should be very little waste and more products of good quality.
Total quality management	This is when all employees in the organisation are committed to achieving quality at all stages. For example, from communication with customers to production of the final products.	All employees are involved in quality. Therefore, there should be no errors in production and no waste.

Outcome 2.3

Outcome 2.3 asks you to explain the costs and benefits of production methods used by large organisations. This is straightforward and some sample answers are given in the table below (remember that costs and benefits can also be advantages and disadvantages):

Production method	Advantages	Disadvantages
Job production	The customer gets exactly what they want and are therefore prepared to pay a high price. They also get a unique product, for example, designer wedding dress, suit, piece of furniture, etc.	Individual products can take a long time to produce and they can be expensive for the customer.

(continued)

Production method	Advantages	Disadvantages
Batch production	Production costs can be reduced as many products are being made at the same time.	If different batches are being made, it can take time to switch machines, therefore, losing some production time.
Flow production	Costs of production are low and many products can be made in a short period.	The product is the same for every customer – nothing is unique.

Outcome 2.4

Outcome 2.4 asks you to describe how current technologies are used in the operations function. Again, this is a straightforward description of the use of current technologies. Some sample answers are given in the table below:

Technology	What this is used for
ICT	ICT can be used for all software applications, for example, spreadsheets to work out production costs, databases to hold stock records, word processing to send letters to suppliers of raw materials, etc.
CAD/CAM	Computer aided design can be used in the design stage of the product to show different views, plans, blueprints, etc. Computer aided manufacture can be used to help with the actual production by using robots and automated systems.
Computerised stock control	This is used to record stock coming into and going out of the organisation. The computer system barcodes items and then adds or subtracts from the database when items are bought and sold. It can produce stock reports and automatically re-order new stock.

This is the end of the section on internal unit assessments for managing marketing and operations. Remember that everything you have learned for these unit assessments is valid and helpful for the final question paper.

However, it is also important to remember that the managing marketing and operations unit has a number of other topics that are not examined in the unit assessments.

Chapter 4: The assignment

The assignment

The assignment that you will produce towards the end of your course is worth 30 marks, which is, of course, 30% of your total mark. This gives you an opportunity to maximise your grade if you put the time and effort into producing an assignment of good quality.

You can start thinking about your assignment at any time during your course but there are some basic principles of planning and preparing that you should follow.

Your teacher or lecturer may give you some guidelines to follow. There are guidelines on the SQA website on how to prepare the assignment. This chapter gives you step-by-step guidance that is easy to follow.

The general advice is that the assignment has two stages. The first stage is planning and gathering evidence that should take you around 6 to 6.5 hours. The second stage is producing the actual report that should take around 1.5 hours. However, this is just guidance. You may take slightly more or less time than this. In addition, you can carry out the two stages at the same time.

1. How to begin the assignment

The first thing you have to do is *choose a business* and decide on a particular issue or problem to investigate. The issue or problem does not have to be very complicated but it should enable you to draw some conclusions and make some recommendations for the business. The choice of business is up to you but some handy hints to follow are:

Top tip

Please note that the assignment must be all your own work.

- Scottish businesses are easy to collect information about and may be known to you.
- Choose a medium to large business that has a website with business or corporate information.

- You can also choose a charity, social enterprise or local government organisation.
- You do not have to contact the business directly but if you know the business or have a relative that works there then this might be helpful.
- Your teacher or lecturer may arrange a visit to a business or may arrange for a speaker from the business to visit your class to give information about the business. However, this is usually just the start of the process – it does not do your assignment for you!

2. Choose a topic or issue or problem to investigate

Here are some examples of suitable topics:

- Pricing strategies
- Environmental issues
- Threat of competition
- Product extension strategies
- Product portfolios
- Mergers, takeovers
- Sources of finance
- Scottish identity
- Promotion and advertising strategies
- Workforce planning – recruitment and selection issues

3. Choose a business analytical tool

You must choose a tool that will be easy for you to report on and that will be suitable for your chosen business. You will have to explain what the analytical technique shows and how it fits in with the topic you have chosen. The most common tools are:

- PESTEC analysis
- Ratio analysis

- SWOT analysis
- Product portfolio analysis (Boston Matrix)

Carrying out the analysis is difficult and you are unlikely to have done anything like this before. Your teacher or lecturer may be able to give you some guidance.

For PESTEC analysis, you would be expected to say how each of the external factors affects your business and what the business has done to try to resolve these issues. However, you must be able to find the evidence of this.

For ratio analysis, you would be expected to calculate ratios for the business using the final accounts that you can find on their website. You would then be expected to comment on each ratio and if possible compare to previous years. Then you would be expected to make recommendations on how to improve each ratio.

A SWOT analysis involves describing the strengths, weaknesses, opportunities and threats for your chosen business – but again, you must be able to provide evidence of this.

A product portfolio analysis can be carried out using the Boston Matrix model.

Here is an example of an approach to using a SWOT analysis:

In this report, I am going to investigate the reasons behind the fall in profits that Tesco have experienced in recent years and what Tesco can do to change this. In this report, the analytical tool I am going to use is a SWOT analysis, which will allow me to identify the strengths of the business. In addition, it will show what makes Tesco one of the leading supermarkets in the UK.

I will also be able to identify Tesco's weaknesses. This will show why Tesco are experiencing a decrease in profits, as well as other problems the company may face. Third, I will identify the opportunities that the business is presented with and any possible opportunities it has not taken advantage of; finally, I will identify the threats the business is faced with and how these threats can affect it.

4. Choose your sources of information

This is the most demanding part of the assignment so far and it is not an easy one! You may choose primary sources – include surveys or questionnaires carried out, interviews with business owners/workers and visiting speakers; or secondary sources – include books, magazines, newspapers, websites, etc. You must have a minimum of two sources.

Some candidates waste a lot of time looking through websites that are of little value or they forget to note down what the source was, so keep a careful note of the websites you have used. For example, you could use a table like the one below:

Source of information	Date used	Summary of information
Business website	15 March	• Aims of the business • Products and services
BBC Business News website	16 March	• Business announces its profits for the year • New law passed by the government that affects businesses
Classroom textbook	17 March	Gave me information on SWOT analysis
Survey of class/family/ teachers	20 March	Gave me opinions on the business products

If you are struggling to find information about your chosen business or chosen topic, you must stop and think again. Perhaps you need to consult your teacher or lecturer and make another choice.

Once you have identified your sources you must name them and say what you used them for and what the value of the source was. This is made clear in the list below:

• Name the research source, for example, survey carried out in class, website address, etc.
• Identify whether the source is primary or secondary.

- Identify why you chose this source, what you used it for and why it was useful in terms of your report.
- Explain the values and limitations of your sources, for example, reliability, validity, relevance, up-to-date, objective, biased, accurate, inaccurate, etc.

Here are some sample answers:

The first research source I used was the business website – www.tesco.com. This is a secondary source of information. I chose this website because it was entirely relevant to my report, as it is the website of the business. I used the website to gather details of the wide range of products that Tesco has for sale. The information was up-to-date and accurate and it give me prices as well. However, some information about the business could be biased in order to attract potential customers. I accessed this website on 15 March 20XX.

The second research source I used was the BBC news site – bbc.co.uk/news. This is a secondary source of information. I chose this website because it contained information about the economy and effects of recession on business. I gathered statistics and graphs to show the number of businesses that went bankrupt during the last five years. This is relevant to my investigation of recession. The BBC news site is reliable, unbiased and up-to-date. I had confidence that the information was from a reliable source as their journalists are employed to be impartial. I accessed this website on 16 March 20XX.

The third research source I used was a survey of my fellow pupils. This is a primary source of information. I used this survey because it enabled me to find out how many people had bought products from my business. I asked three questions in my survey about quality, price and if they would buy again from the business. The results of my survey are shown in the graphs in appendix 1. My survey is reliable, relevant and it is first-hand information. I am confident that the answers to my survey questions were honest and truthful. I carried out this survey on 17 March 20XX.

Top tip

You should make sure that all of your sources of information are listed in your appendices at the end of your report.

5. Carry out your analysis and interpretation of your findings

You must make it very clear to the examiner what you have found from your research and what it means for your topic and business. You can then make conclusions and recommendations. There are some key phrases you can use that clearly indicate that you have researched and found the information yourself.

- From my research source I found out that...
- From the website I noticed that...
- The results of my survey indicated that...
- You can see clearly from my graphs that...
- I noticed that the customer feedback page had three unhappy customers...
- The ratings on TripAdvisor indicated that...
- The article that I read in the newspaper proves that...
- I am confident that these figures mean that...

Some examples of using these phrases are detailed below:

From my research source 1 (the business website) I found out that...

Pricing strategies used vary from one season of the year to another according to customer demand for certain products. For example, in summer, there is more demand for cold drinks and ice cream; therefore, these products were selected for a low pricing strategy from May to September. During the winter months, prices are increased again.

From my research source 2 (survey) I found out that:

- *25% of customers had complained in the last three months*
- *45% of customers had complained in the last two months*
- *30% of customers had complained in the last month*

This is shown is the graph/pie chart. This means that the business is not meeting customer needs and must address the issues that customers are complaining about quickly in order to restore confidence in the business.

From my research source 3 (newspaper article) I found out that the PESTEC factors surrounding the decline in holidays taken in the UK were…

Political. The government had not increased the minimum wage rate very much in the last two years. Therefore, families did not have enough money to go on holiday.

Economic. Unemployment figures showed that there were large numbers of people out of work who could not afford to go on holiday.

Social. More and more people enjoy holidays abroad rather than staying in the UK.

Technological. Mobile devices, laptops, etc. make it easier to stay in touch on holiday abroad.

Environment. The weather in the UK can be disappointing in the summer so many people choose to holiday abroad.

Competition. There is so much choice in terms of tour companies that prices are very competitive.

Graphs and charts in your research section or in the appendices

Graphs and charts are extremely effective in demonstrating the results of your findings from surveys or other statistical information. However, make sure you get the most from your graphs and charts by following the golden rules.

1. Your graph or chart must have a heading.
2. You must label the axis – x and y.
3. You must have a key (sometimes referred to as the legend).
4. You must have data labels or percentages in a pie chart.
5. Your graph or chart must be accurate.

Here is a properly labelled chart:

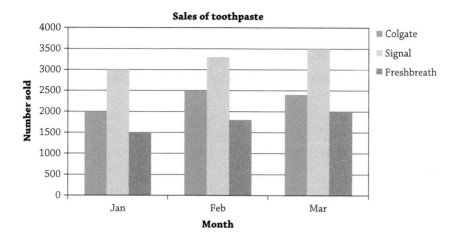

6. Make your conclusions and recommendations based on your findings

You should now try to sum up your evidence and make your conclusions or recommendations. Again, there are key phrases you can use, for example:

- I have concluded that XXX business should…
- I suggest that the business does…
- Summing up my evidence, the conclusions I can make are…
- I would recommend that the business does the following…
- The business should think about doing…
- The course of action the business should now take is to…
- The business should offer…

However, each conclusion or recommendation should be based on your evidence and have a justification or explanation of the effect it will have, for example:

Based on the findings from the business website, I suggest that the business conducts training for its employees on customer service. This should mean that the number of complaints reduce and that customers will be happy to return and shop there again.

The course of action that the business should now take is to expand their product range to appeal to an older segment of the market, for example, the 65 to 75 age group. This will address the lack of sales to customers in this sector of the market.

I recommend that the business employ more staff in the operations department to carry out quality assurance. Quality assurance checks will mean that fewer problems are identified at the end of the production process and there will be no need for product recalls in the future.

There are 8 marks allocated for this section. You could aim for eight separate conclusions and recommendations or you could aim for four and write an extended response for each one to gain the 8 marks.

7. Prepare your report

You should use the headings given in the assignment advice, which are given below:

Introduction – 3 marks
This must include the topic being investigated and the name of your business. You should also include the name of the analytical tool being used.

Research – 4 marks
You must provide a minimum of two sources that can be primary, secondary or both. You must identify the source, say why you have used it and outline the value of the source or why it is relevant to your report.

Analysis and interpretation – 12 marks

You must make a number of analytical or interpretative comments based on your research findings. You can have more than one finding from a piece of research. You must also link your findings or interpretations to your business analytical tool.

Conclusions and recommendations – 8 marks

You must come to conclusions or make recommendations based on your findings. **There should be no new or additional information in this section.**

Collating and reporting – 3 marks

You must make sure that your final report looks professional and is organised. The marks are allocated as follows:

- Headings – 1 mark
- Use of business terminology – 1 mark
- Report being an appropriate length – 1 mark

Appendices

You may include up to four appendices but these are not marked. However, these will be read by the examiner and they will give an overall impression of your assignment so take time to make sure they are organised and accurate.

Final points

- Your report should be word processed.
- Stick to the suggested page length, which is no more than six pages.

Top tip

Top tips to maximise your assignment marks:

- Choose a business with lots of online information – website, Facebook page, newspaper reports.
- Choose a topic and analytical tool that you are comfortable with.
- Plan your research – note down sources you have used and why you have used them.
- Organise your thoughts – what information have you found and what does it mean?
- Plan to use a survey – surveys are a good way to prove you have researched and analysed your findings.
- Use charts or graphs to display your survey findings.
- Use interpretative or analytical comments such as 'I found from reading the newspaper article that...'
- Organise all your findings at the end.
- Use the recommended headings for your report.
- Include all the relevant appendices.
- Give yourself plenty of time to avoid rushing at the end.

- These pages should be 1.5 spacing and be a reasonable size font, for example, 11 or 12 point.
- Include appendices that should be no more than four pages in length and they can include tables, graphs and charts; as well as lists of websites, books, articles, etc.
- Make sure that you reference the appendices so that it is clear to what research you are referring.

Your total report should be no more than **10 pages**. You will lose marks if your report is too long.

Chapter 5: The final examination

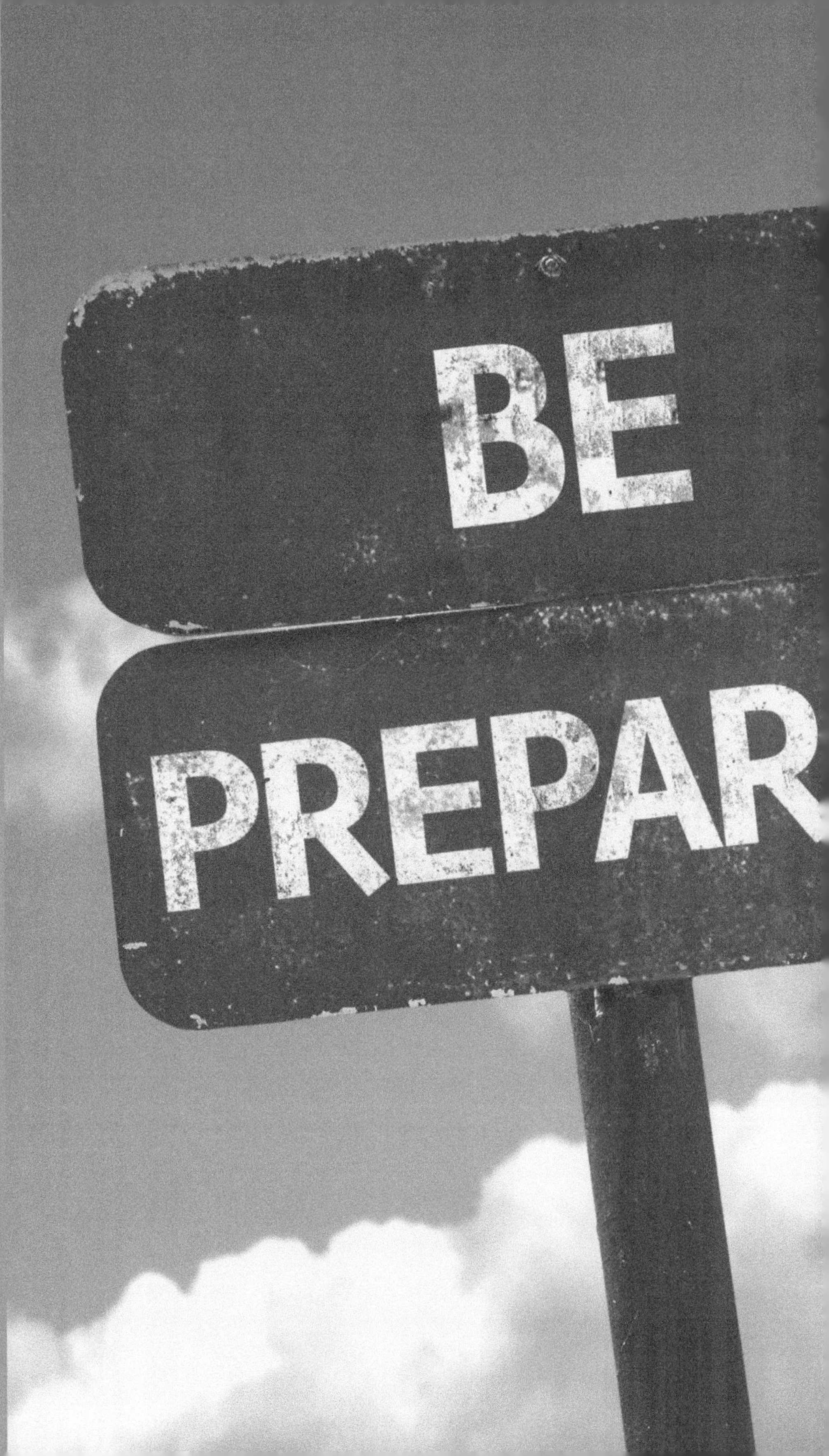

The final examination

The final examination is often referred to as the question paper. This is because your whole course is made up of two pieces of work – the *assignment* (30 marks) and the *question paper* (70 marks). The question paper will cover topics from the whole of the course but remember that everything you have already learned for the unit assessments and the assignment will still be of help to you.

To achieve a grade A pass in the whole course you need to score more than 70% overall. This is a combined score between your assignment and your question paper. The more marks you can achieve in the assignment the better!

The exam lasts for 2 hours and 15 minutes and it has two sections. Section 1 has a case study (sometimes called stimulus material). You have to read the case study carefully and answer questions based on this to the value of 30 marks.

Section 2 has four questions that can be from any section of the course. Each question is worth 10 marks but this is normally broken down into smaller parts, for example, 1a for 4 marks, 1b for 2 marks and 1c for 4 marks.

Therefore, it makes sense to make sure you spread your time evenly between both sections.

Preparing for the final exam

What is the best approach for the exam? Everyone is different but there are some general principles that will help you before the exam day.

1. Practise as many previous examination papers as you can before your final exam

Your teacher or lecturer will be able to help you source these and each year the exam is added onto the SQA website. Here are some examples from the SQA.

2015 Higher question paper – Google

The case study gave a very detailed account of the growth and development of Google over the last 15 years. There was a timeline that illustrated the history of the business as well as detailed financial information. Here is the timeline:

Exhibit 1 — Google's timeline

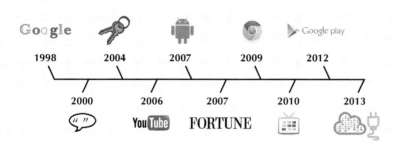

1998 — Google.com
Google.com is registered as a domain.

2000 — Google in 10 Languages
The first 10 languages of Google are released. Today, search is available in 150+ languages.

2004 — Move to new HQ
Google move to their Mountainview headquarters, 11 years before the move to their latest "Googleplex" HQ.

2006 — YouTube acquired
Google announce the takeover of YouTube.

2007 — Android
Google launch Android — the first open platform for smartphone devices.

2007 — "Fortune" Best Company to Work For
Google is rated no 1 company to work for in a well-known business magazine.

2009 — Google Chrome
Google launch their own web browser, Google Chrome.

2010 — Google TV
Google TV is launched.

2012 — Google Play
Android Market is rebranded Google Play, a digital content store offering apps, games, books, music and more.

2013 — Energy efficiency in the cloud
Google funded research shows that increased use of cloud computing would drastically reduce energy consumption.

SQA specimen paper – J Sainsbury's

The case study gave information on the vision and values of the business as well as comprehensive information on their growth and marketing strategy. There was also financial information in a table that was given in order to ask questions about ratio analysis. Here is an extract from the paper:

Further information

Exhibit 1 — Extract from Sainsbury's financial performance

	2012/13	2011/12	Change
	£ millions	*£ millions*	%
Sales	23,303	22,294	+ 4·5
Gross Profit	829	789	+ 5·1
Net Profit	614	598	+ 2.7

Source: Adapted from J. Sainsbury PLC Annual Report 2013

Exhibit 2 — Sainsbury's market share

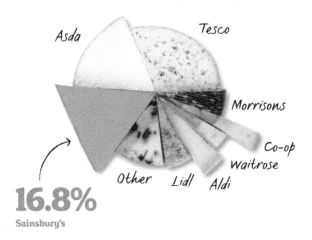

16.8%
Sainsbury's

Source: Kantar Worldpanel total till roll for the 52 weeks to 17 March 2013

SQA exemplar paper – Peter Scott Ltd and Gloverall

The case study gave information about the business as well as detailed information on their production strategy, their brands and marketing including the Boston Matrix. The information on the Boston Matrix was interesting as the model was provided for you to use so that you could comment on the products of the business. Here is an extract from the paper:

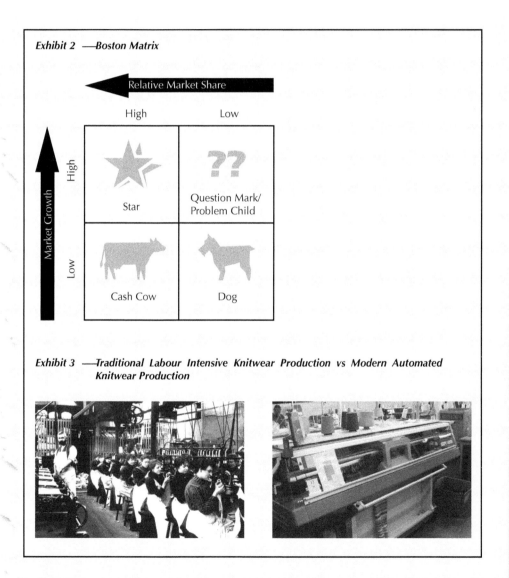

Exhibit 2 ——Boston Matrix

Exhibit 3 ——Traditional Labour Intensive Knitwear Production vs Modern Automated Knitwear Production

As you can see from the three examples above, the case study can be very different each year. Therefore, it is important that you read the case study carefully making notes as you go along or underlining important pieces of information. Then read the questions that relate to the case study. It is wise to read the full case study again and this time try to highlight where you will find information relating to each question.

You can find more examples of exam papers in Leckie & Leckie's *CfE Higher Business Management Practice Papers for SQA Exams*.

Top tip

It is also a good idea to extend your reading over the course of the year – reading business articles in newspapers, reading corporate information on business websites and listening to the business news whenever you can.

2. Look at the marking instructions for each exam paper

These are provided on the SQA website and whilst they are intended to help teachers, they are of help to students to guide you on answering. Also, look at the marks allocated for each question. Each mark represents a full sentence. Six marks = six sentences, which could mean three-quarters of a page of writing.

3. Remember the command words

They are extremely important and your answers should take into account the command word being used.

4. Practise reading from reliable business websites

These should have company or corporate information. For example, major supermarkets have corporate information that can be easily accessed. See the websites for Tesco, Sainsbury's, Morrisons; also Greggs, Baxters, AG Barr, etc.

5. Use proper sentences and use business terminology

At this stage, you should avoid one-word answers and avoid bullet points. Bullet points are unlikely to have the detail required to provide sophisticated answers.

The day of the exam

Section 1: the case study

Read the case study carefully and highlight any important points. You may want to read the case study again to get a very clear idea of the business and the information you have gathered.

Look at the questions and try to make the link between the question being asked and the relevant information in the case study. You could use a coding system – for example, annotate the case study with a circled 1 for question 1, 2 for question 2, etc.

When answering questions it is acceptable to lift information directly from the case study. This is really important as it demonstrates that you have read and understood the case study.

Here is an example from the 2015 Higher question paper:

Q **Explain** the benefits of Google's corporate culture to the organisation and its employees. **4 marks**

Corporate Culture

Google has a very relaxed corporate culture and this has been taken into account in the planning of the building. Although employees can work from outwith the office, the new HQ has been designed to encourage employees to want to be there so that they benefit from regular communication and idea sharing. Most Google employees have flexible working hours, adding to the general feeling of wellbeing.

The design will also allow employees to meet up easily and chat. Employees can wear their own casual clothes and pedal on free bicycles or walk to informal meetings in the roof gardens or coffee shops. The Googleplex will continue to use the preferred Google colour scheme of primary colours currently used in the existing HQ and will house impressive facilities. Google's offices are well known for their perks such as gourmet cafes, sleep pods, laptops attached to gym equipment and even pool tables and bowling alleys!

A good answer to this question would be:

The benefits of Google's corporate culture to the organisation are as follows:

Employees have demonstrated that they want to be present in the building rather than work from home as they can communicate regularly and share ideas. This is a benefit to Google as this means that employees will be more motivated to work harder and idea sharing usually leads to more positive results and increased productivity.

Most employees have flexible working hours, adding to the general feeling of wellbeing. This is a benefit to Google because this means that feelings of wellbeing can lead to increased loyalty to the business and better quality of work.

Employees can wear their own casual clothes. This is a benefit to employees as this means that they will feel more comfortable and will not have to spend extra money on 'work clothes', which they might not wear otherwise.

Employees can take advantage of gourmet cafes, sleep pods, gym equipment, pool tables and bowling alleys. This is a benefit to employees as this means that they will feel trusted and that they can take some time out to relax and enjoy themselves. This will also lead to a reduction in the stress levels of employees.

> **Top tip**
>
> Note the use of the linking phrase *'this means that'* to demonstrate that you are actually giving an explanation.

Here is an example from the SQA specimen paper:

> **Q** **Describe**, using evidence from the information provided, ethical and environmental factors Sainsbury's has taken into account. **5 marks**

Source raw materials with integrity — by ensuring our products ensure sustainability, for example, responsibly caught seafood and no contribution to global deforestation.

Reduce consumption of unhealthy foods — by providing clear nutritional information.

Respect our environment — by reducing carbon emissions and continuing to use solar energy.

Be a great place to work — by providing certificated training for employees.

Make a positive difference to the community — by encouraging children to enjoy physical activity.

A good answer to this question would be:

From the case study, I can provide the following evidence to show what ethical and environmental factors Sainsbury's has taken into account.

The first factor I would like to describe is an ethical factor. Ethical means doing the right thing. Sainsbury's source their raw materials from sustainable sources. This means that the source will not be depleted and it can be used over again. They catch seafood responsibly to ensure that other fish stocks are not damaged. They do not contribute to deforestation, which means they replenish any trees by planting new ones.

The second ethical factor I would like to describe is encouraging customers to eat healthy meals. Sainsbury's provide nutritional information on all their food products so that customers can make informed food choices about what is healthy and what is not.

The third ethical factor I would like to describe is motivating employees in order to make them feel more valued. Sainsbury's offer training to their employees. This will make them better at their jobs and reduce their stress. It will also improve the quality of their work.

The fourth ethical factor I would like to describe is contributing to the local community. Sainsbury's take part in community activities that encourage children to be active and play actively. This contributes to their overall health and fitness.

The environmental factor I would like to describe is that Sainsbury's try to help the environment by reducing carbon emissions and using solar power. This will help reduce energy consumption overall, thus saving valuable resources.

Top tip

Note that there are more than five proper sentences in this answer to earn 5 marks.

Here is an example from the SQA exemplar paper:

Q **Discuss** the use of just-in-time for Peter Scott & Co. **4 marks**

The management of Gloverall has invested in modern technology to improve the process, making use of just-in-time production at the Hawick factory. The old machinery, which relied heavily on skilled staff, has been replaced with new automated machines. This has resulted in a change to the staff skills required at the Hawick factory.

A good answer to this question would be:

In discussing the use of just-in-time for Peter Scott & Co, I would like to outline the advantages and disadvantages.

The advantage of using just-in-time production is that capital is not tied up in stock; however, the disadvantage is that there is always the risk that raw materials will not arrive in time, which may hold up production.

The advantage of using just-in-time is that it reduces the need for warehouse stock and space; however, the disadvantage is that the business can lose out on bulk buying discounts.

The advantage of using just-in-time is that it reduces the cost of warehouse staff; however, the disadvantage is that there is an increase in delivery costs as supplies are received on a more regular basis.

The advantage of using just-in-time is that it reduces the possibility that stock can be damaged or deteriorate; however, the disadvantage is that stock may have to be used as soon as it arrives, therefore, there is not always time to check the quality of stock.

The advantage of using just-in-time is that it reduces the need for large stocks to be held, which means the business can respond quickly to changes in taste and fashion; however, the disadvantage is that they need to have very reliable suppliers who charge reasonable prices.

Top tip

Note the link between each sentence that shows the advantage and disadvantage. This is more than enough for 4 marks.

Section 2

There is no choice in section 2 so you can attempt the questions in any order you like. Just remember to show clearly what question you are answering.

Usually, each question is devoted to a particular topic or unit. For example, question 1 may be all about finance, question 2 may be all about marketing.

The same advice applies:

- Look at the command words – underline each command word in each question.
- Look at the marks allocation.
- Answer in sentences.
- Avoid bullet points.
- Use business terminology.

Here are some examples of section 2 questions from the 2015 Higher exam paper:

 Discuss the advantages and disadvantages of centralised stock storage.　**4 marks**

A good answer to this question would be:

An advantage of centralised stock storage is that only specialist authorised staff will issue stock from the storage area whereas a disadvantage of non-centralised stock storage is that anyone can issue stock. This makes it more difficult to keep a track of where the stock is.

An advantage of centralised stock storage is that it is more cost effective to have one storage area for small items of stock whereas a disadvantage is that small items of stock spread throughout the business can lead to loss of stock items.

An advantage of centralised stock storage is that stock items can be re-ordered when required so no excess stock is held whereas a disadvantage of centralised stock storage is that the same stock item could be ordered by several different departments at the same time leading to an excess of stock that may not get used up by the correct date.

An advantage of centralised stock storage is that the delivery and receipt of stock can be checked in one place for errors or omissions immediately whereas a disadvantage of stock being delivered to several different departments is that it is difficult to trace errors or omissions immediately across several different departments.

Look at how each section of this answer has been linked together to make it a proper discussion.

Q **Describe** the sales promotions that could be used when launching a new product.

4 marks

Sales promotions that could be used when launching a new product are:

1. *Celebrity endorsement. This is when the business asks a famous person to endorse their product by appearing in advertisements and publicity events for the product. Most often, the celebrity says they have used the product and they usually give the benefits of using the product.*

2. *Special offers. This is when the business offers customers deals, for example, buy one get one free or buy two and get a third half price. The main element of any deal is that the customer does not pay full price.*

3. *Competition entry. This is when the business promises to enter the customer into a free competition once they have purchased the product. The main element of this is that you must buy the product first so the business ensures they have the custom.*

4. *Trials or free samples. This is when the business gives the customer a sample of the product to try out for free. It could be free tasting, for example, in the supermarket or an actual sample to take home and use. Alternatively, the customer could get to use the product for a trial period to see what they think of it.*

There is not a clear set of words that can be used for a describe question. In the answer above, the nearest is the use of *'this is when'* to describe what the promotion is.

Describe one theory of motivation used by managers.   **3 marks**

This question comes from the **managing people** section of the course and it was not asked in the unit assessments. There are several possible theories you can choose for this answer – Maslow's Hierarchy of Needs model, McGregor's Theory X and Theory Y and Hertzberg's theory. Only one theory has been chosen here for illustration purposes.

A good answer to this question would be:

Maslow's Hierarchy of Needs theory is based on the idea that employees have needs, which have to be met at work, but that these needs are in a hierarchy and that the most basic needs must be satisfied first before moving on to the next set of needs. The most basic needs are food and water and these are referred to as physiological needs. The next needs are to feel safe and protected and these are called safety needs. After this, employees need to feel a sense of belonging and to be valued. These are called social needs. After this, employees become more developed and need to feel self-esteem, be recognised and have some status. This is called esteem needs. At the highest level, employees need to feel they have fulfilled their potential. This is called self-actualization and these needs are the most complex to meet.

Compare the use of penetration pricing with skimming pricing.   **3 marks**

This is a compare question so you have to show the similarities and the differences between the two. This question is from the **marketing** section of the course and it was not asked in the unit assessments.

A good answer for this question would be:

Penetration pricing is used in a highly competitive market whereas *skimming pricing is used in a market with little or no competition.*

Penetration pricing means that the product will be introduced at a low price whereas *skimming pricing means that the product is introduced at a high price.*

With penetration pricing, the price will be increased once the product has been established whereas *with skimming pricing, the price is decreased as competition enters the market.*

Top tip

Note three separate points with the distinguishing word '*whereas*'.

Q **Explain** the benefits of using information technology to deliver staff training.

3 marks

This is an explain question; therefore, it requires reasons to be given. Explain the benefits means saying how the use of IT will make staff training better.

A good answer for this question would be:

The first benefit of using IT to deliver staff training is that presentation software can be used to give a visual as well as an audio presentation. Graphs, pictures, sounds and video can make the presentation more enjoyable. This means that *staff attention can be captured and that staff can absorb the information in a variety of different ways. If staff can access the presentation across an intranet, they will have a reminder of the presentation at any time.*

The second benefit of using IT to deliver staff training is that staff do not have to be present in the same room to experience the training. The presentation can take place using web conferencing, therefore *reducing the need to travel. The presentation can also* be emailed to those who have missed the training; *therefore* making sure that nobody misses out.

The third benefit of using IT to deliver staff training is that the training may be linked to online learning courses that chart or record the progress of the member of staff. *This means that* both the manager and the employee can see the progress being made and they can be offered online tutorial support. *Therefore* the employee never needs to feel that they do not understand what is being delivered.

Top tip

Note three separate points with the use of *'therefore'* to explain how things are better.

Here are some sample questions from the SQA exemplar paper:

Q | **Describe** the possible methods of growth for a public limited company. **5 marks**

This is a fairly straightforward description question from the **understanding business** unit. If you have learned this section, it is a good question to pick up 5 marks.

A good answer for this question would be:

Vertical integration – this is when organisations at a different stage in the same industry combine. This can be backward vertical integration or forward vertical integration. Backward is towards the raw materials and forward is towards the point of purchase by the customer. Some examples are if a supermarket buys over a dairy farm to ensure a supply of milk, cheese and other dairy products or a retailer buys over a manufacturer, for example, a shoe shop buys over the shoe factory.

Conglomerate integration or diversification – this is when completely unrelated businesses merge or combine. A good example is Unilever, which produces ice cream, cleaning products and shampoo.

De-integration/de-merger – this is when businesses that have previously merged decide to go their own way again in order to concentrate on what they are good at, for example, Cadbury's and Schweppes decided to de-merge for this reason.

Organic growth – this is when a business increases the number of products sold or the number of outlets that it has but it happens as a result of increases in demand rather than a strategic decision to become very large.

Merger or takeover – this is when two businesses agree to become one by either agreement (merger) or when one business takes over a smaller one (takeover).

Top tip

There are more points here than the 5 marks so this answer is more than required. However, just a list of the methods would not be acceptable.

Q **Explain** the impact of industrial action on an organisation. **4 marks**

This question asks you to explain the impact of industrial action. Remember explaining the impact means saying how it is better or worse.

A good answer for this question would be:

If employees go on strike then they refuse to carry out their work and this means that no products or services are sold or produced. This means that the business can lose customers.

If employees have an overtime ban then they refuse to work any extra hours, therefore orders can be late, which means that customers may go elsewhere.

Employees can go on a 'go slow', which means that they work at a slower rate than normal, which can increase the costs of production. This can also mean that orders are late and customers will be unhappy.

Employees can have a 'sit in' where they do not work while remaining at their workplace, which means that employers cannot bring in other staff to do their work.

Employees can undertake a 'work to rule', which means that **they only undertake the tasks that are in their contract.** *This means that* **some jobs are not done at all and it might give the business a bad reputation.**

Employees can 'picket' the business, which means that **they try to prevent others from entering the business to do their jobs. Picketing can be very stressful for employees who are not involved in the dispute and for any customers trying to access the business.**

Top tip

This answer gives more points than asked for but note how the phrase *'this means that'* is used over and again to show the impact.

Improving your exam technique for section 1

Here are some examples of stimulus material and questions based on the SQA exemplar paper:

Present Situation

Despite having an excellent reputation and strong brand, Peter Scott & Co. suffered heavily from increased overseas competition. This resulted in the 120 redundancies and forced the company directors to work closely with local and national government agencies to save the remaining jobs. The Scottish Government attempted to help the company directors by setting up discussions with several parties who had an interest in purchasing the company.

Gloverall's Plans for Peter Scott & Co.

Gloverall's Finance Director, Walter Goulding, suggested that it wanted to rebuild the workforce saying, "We are continuing to employ the initial 20 people from Peter Scott & Co., but will look to build back up the local workforce". He added, "The administrators had decimated the workforce. There were no knitters or production staff left which left us in a poor situation to begin with. But the Peter Scott brand is an excellent product and we want to get production up to full speed again in Hawick as soon as possible. The 'Made in Scotland' label is very important to our future success".

Here is a describe question from this paper with an example of a weak answer:

Q | **Describe** how workforce planning could ensure that Peter Scott & Co. has appropriate staff. **4 marks**

Peter Scott & Co. have made 120 staff redundant recently. They are working with the Scottish Government to save the remaining jobs. There are no knitters or production staff, which has left them in a poor situation. They need more employees to get production up to full speed again. They will need to advertise to try and attract more employees back to the company.

This is a very weak answer as it has not described any workforce planning tools. At best this answer has re-stated the problems being faced by the company. At the end of the answer it says to advertise to try and attract more workers, this would possibly receive 1 mark.

A much better answer would be:

The workforce planning tools that Peter Scott & Co. could use to ensure appropriate staff are described below:

Skills analysis. This involves carrying out an analysis or survey of all the skills that existing employees already have. These should then be matched to the requirements of all the jobs available and any gaps identified. If there are skills missing that current employees do not have the company should try and recruit new employees with these additional skills or retrain existing staff in these new skills.

Staffing forecast. This involves estimating how many staff will be needed for future production orders. They will need to know which times of the year they are going to be producing more than usual and which times of the year they will produce less than usual. Staffing requirements should then be worked out on this basis and temporary employees taken on as required.

Outsourcing or sub-contracting. This involves using an outside company to carry out parts of the work that Peter Scott & Co. cannot do, either because they don't have enough employees or they don't have enough employees with the particular skills needed. An outside business will then agree to do the work and Peter Scott & Co. would pay them for this.

Change working patterns. This involves introducing different working patterns for existing employees and new employees, flexible working hours, temporary contracts and part-time contracts for example. This means that staffing levels can be adjusted when required for busy periods of production and quieter periods.

This is a much better answer as it has described four workforce planning tools and this answer would now be awarded 4 marks.

Here is another extract from the from the SQA exemplar paper:

Exhibit 1 – Peter Scott & Co. Brand Range

Golf Knitwear – Peter Scott & Co. offers an extensive range of exclusive, personalized knitwear for both men and lady golfers. Available for custom logo embroidery, Peter Scott knitwear is ideal for golf societies, golf club cresting and corporate golf days.

Fashion Knitwear – Peter Scott & Co. combines quality and craftsmanship with innovation and design. All garments are crafted in its factory in Hawick, and include a new range for both summer and winter.

The question relating to this section is as follows:

Q **Exhibit 1** shows that Peter Scott & Co. has a range of new products. Describe the pricing strategies that Peter Scott & Co. could use to launch these products. **6 marks**

The pricing strategies that Peter Scott & Co. could use to launch these products are:

Cost Plus Pricing. This is when an amount is added onto the price to cover costs.

Competitive Pricing. This is when the price is set the same as similar products.

High Pricing. This is when a high price is set to sell the product.

This is an example of a weak answer as the descriptions are very vague. At best this answer would be awarded 3 marks.

A much better answer would be:

The pricing strategies that Peter Scott & Co. could use to launch these products are:

Cost Plus Pricing. This is when the business firstly works out the cost of the product being produced. Then they decide to add on a percentage mark-up for profit. The percentage can be based on the level of profit they want or what is the usual mark-up for their industry. The mark-up also includes the amount they will have to pay for advertising the product. The percentage mark-up can be increased or decreased at any time in order to stimulate sales. This is an easy and straightforward method of pricing goods where the cost can easily be worked out.

Competitive Pricing. This is when the business looks at the prices of other products which are similar and then sets their prices at the same level. For example, Peter Scott would look at the prices of other golfing jumpers. This allows customers to make decisions based on the style and brand image of the product and it also helps to prevent a price war.

High pricing. This is when the business decides to set the price of the product at a high price or higher than others in the same market. This high price is set throughout the whole of the life of the product and gives the impression of good quality and/or a good brand image. In the case of Peter Scott the image will be good quality wool which is made in Scotland. Some customers are happy to pay high prices if they think they are getting a premium product.

This is a much better answer as there are much fuller descriptions of the three pricing strategies. This answer would now be awarded the full 6 marks.

Here is a third extract from the SQA exemplar paper:

Alistair Young, Operations Manager at Peter Scott & Co. said "The 'Learning Working Earning' initiative is definitely of major interest to us. Thankfully, with the rise in demand for authentic Scottish Produce, we have seen a fantastic growth in trade with our sales up by 30% in the last two years. This means we are now in a position to expand our workforce".

A question relating to this section could be:

Describe the role of the Operations Manager within Peter Scott & Co.

5 marks

The role of the Operations Manager within Peter Scott & Co. is to give commands. They have to make employees aware of their tasks and aims. They would need to plan and be organized as to how many jumpers they were going to produce. They would have to co-ordinate with employees and make sure everyone is doing the tasks they are supposed to be doing.

This is an example of a weak answer with repetition. The answer really only makes reference to the number of jumpers to be produced.

The role of the manager can be summed up with five key words – planning, organising, commanding, communicating and controlling (POCCC).

This answer can be improved as below:

The role of the manager within Operations at Peter Scott & Co. is to make sure that production flows smoothly. The manager will have to plan for production by making sure that all the raw materials are purchased in time, that equipment is all in good working order and that all employees are trained properly. The manager does not have to do all these things by themselves, they can organize others such as supervisors to help them.

The manager has to make sure that each employee is given the appropriate 'commands' or instructions so that they are very clear which tasks they have to complete and when they must be completed by.

The manager also has to communicate with all employees in order to be aware of any problems. This can be done through meetings, text messages, memos, or notice boards.

They also have to communicate with suppliers in case there are raw materials missing or they are not of good quality.

The manager must also control the flow of production and check the quality of the finished goods. This can be done by quality control or by total quality management.

This is now a much better answer as it gives at least five separate points that the manager should undertake and it also relates to operations. This answer would now be awarded 5 marks.

Here is another possible question about Peter Scott & Co.:

Q **Describe** the costs and benefits of promotional activities that could be used by Peter Scott & Co. to sell their products. **6 marks**

One promotional method they could use is celebrity endorsement. This is when high profile celebrities or golfers could endorse the products by wearing them and this will make everyone want to buy them. Another promotional method they could use is advertising the golfing jumpers on the TV. This way everyone who plays golf will see the jumpers and might buy them.

This is a weak answer as only one promotional method has been described and this is celebrity endorsement, the rest of the answer refers to advertising. Mixing up promotion and advertising is a common error. In addition it has only mentioned one of the benefits of celebrity endorsement and not any of the costs. This answer will only receive 1 mark.

A much better answer would be:

One promotional method Peter Scott & Co. could use is celebrity endorsement. This is when high profile celebrities or golfers endorse the jumpers by wearing them when they play golf. One benefit of this is that the jumpers will become more popular. However one cost is that celebrities usually get paid large sums of money to do this.

Another promotional method they could use is free competition entry. They could offer a prize of a round of golf at a famous golf course, or a chance to meet a famous golfer. One benefit of this is that more customers may be attracted by the chance to play golf. However the costs are that the company still has to pay for the prize and the number of extra customers attracted by the offer might be very small.

Another promotional method they could use is BOGOF offers, such as buy-one-get-one-free or buy-one-get-one-at-a-reduced-price. One benefit of this is that customers like to get something for free and so this usually attracts more customers. However one cost is that customers might be put off if they think that the fact that the products are being given away for free means that they are inferior.

This is a much better answer as it mentions three different promotional methods and clearly describes one cost and one benefit for each. This answer would now be awarded the full 6 marks.

Improving your exam technique for section 2

In section 2 of the exam paper you have no choice about which questions you answer – you should answer them all. However, you can attempt the questions in any order you wish. Just make sure you have clearly labelled your answers.

Here are some examples of past paper questions with weak answers given. Below each weak answer, advice is given on how to improve the answer.

| Q | **Discuss** the use of outsourcing. | **5 marks** |

Outsourcing is where a business outsources so that experts and specialists do the work to a higher standard. The organisation does not have the correct equipment to carry out the work; therefore, the quality may be poor. Fewer workers are needed in the business when work is outsourced.

This answer is very weak and it does not really address the command word discuss. The answer does not make it very clear what the advantages and disadvantages of outsourcing are. At most, this question would be awarded 2 marks.

A much better answer would be:

Outsourcing is where a business sends out work to another company or individual to complete on their behalf.

The first advantage of outsourcing is that the work can be carried out by experts or specialists and this usually means the work is of a high standard.

The second advantage of outsourcing is that the business carrying out the work will have the correct equipment to do the work; therefore, the work can be completed in a reasonable time and to a high quality.

The third advantage of outsourcing is that the business can let some staff go, which will reduce their labour costs.

However, one disadvantage of outsourcing is that the outsourced work can be very expensive to complete.

A second disadvantage is that the outsourced business may not be reliable and may not complete the work on time or they may not understand the particular requirements of the job.

This answer provides three advantages and two disadvantages and will therefore be awarded 5 marks.

Q **Describe** the four main stages of the product life cycle.   **4 marks**

The four main stages of the product life cycle are introduction, growth, maturity and decline. Introduction is when the product is introduced, growth is when the product grows, maturity is when the produce matures and decline is when the product does not sell any more.

This is a very weak answer indeed. In fact, it will receive no marks. The candidate has only named the four stages of the product life cycle and has just said the same thing twice over. There are no descriptions contained in this answer.

A much better answer would be:

The first stage of the product life cycle is introduction. This is when the product first enters the market for sale. It is not very well known and sales are usually low.

The second stage of the product life cycle is growth. This is when the product becomes better known through advertising and more customers buying the product. Sales begin to increase as the product expands into the market.

The third stage of the product life cycle is maturity. This is when sales reach their maximum as there are no new customers to buy the product. This stage can last for a long time.

The fourth stage of the product life cycle is decline. This is when sales start to fall as customers go elsewhere to buy other products and the product loses its popularity.

This is a much better answer as it clearly describes each stage of the product life cycle. This answer would be awarded 4 marks.

Q **Explain** the advantages of staff training for an organisation.   **4 marks**

Staff training is when employees are trained in their jobs. This training can be carried out on-the-job or off-the-job. On-the-job training is when an employee is trained by someone else in the business who is good at this job. Off-the-job training is when the employee goes to college or university and may gain additional qualifications.

This is a very weak answer and makes the classic mistake of not answering the question. This answer has attempted to describe staff training and it has not explained the advantages at all. This answer would not receive any marks.

A much better answer is as follows:

Staff training has many advantages for an organisation. The first advantage is that employees will feel more confident to carry out their jobs. This means that fewer mistakes will be made and that customers will be happy. The overall image of the organisation will improve.

The second advantage is that employees will be more productive as they will be more skilled. This means that profits will increase and that customers will get a speedy service.

The third advantage is that staff will be more motivated and may wish to apply for promotion. This means that staff absence and staff turnover could be reduced, as staff are committed to the organisation that trains them.

The fourth advantage is that staff who have been trained will be able to train others in the organisation. This means that the organisation can reduce spending on external training and not have to pay for cover for employees who are away on training courses.

This answer has given four advantages and it has used the key phrase *'this means that'* in order to show their explanation. This answer will receive the full 4 marks.

Chapter 6: Common pitfalls

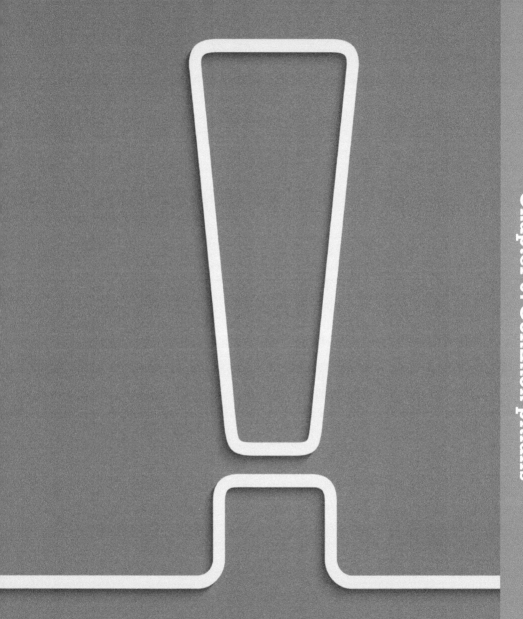

Common pitfalls

Almost every candidate experiences exam nerves and can make silly mistakes during the exam. However, there are a number of common pitfalls for Higher Business Management that you should try to avoid.

1. Read the case study carefully

You must spend time reading the case study – you will be asked questions that relate directly to this. It is acceptable to use the wording of the case study so underline or highlight sections that you think are important.

2. Read the questions carefully

Underline the command word for the question and answer accordingly. It is very common for candidates to describe instead of explain or to use bullet points instead of a proper discussion – make sure you are very clear in your answer.

3. Look at the marks allocation

Take a note of the marks allocated and answer accordingly. A 5-mark question needs at least five proper sentences. It is very rare for any question to be answered properly with just one or two sentences.

4. Keep note of your time allocation

You have two sections in your exam but remember that you should spread your time evenly between both sections. Section 1 is worth 30 marks but you need time to read the case study. Section 2 is worth 40 marks. Make sure you leave enough time to answer all of section 2.

5. Use business terminology

Make sure your answers reflect the business knowledge that you have by using proper business terminology and sophisticated language. For example, the word money is often used incorrectly. Instead of 'money', be clear about what you mean. Possible references are:

- Profit – the business has made a profit on buying goods and selling them at a higher price.
- Capital – the owners have raised more capital by selling more shares.
- Revenue – the business has increased sales revenue by increasing the selling price or sales volume.

You should keep a 'business dictionary' throughout your study of Higher Business Management and note down commonly used business phrases. For example, sectors of the economy, the four factors of production, desk research and field research, the seven Ps of the marketing mix, quality control, quality assurance, total quality management, etc.

6. Make sure you prepare thoroughly

To make sure you can boost your grade to an A pass, you must work steadily throughout the year. Do not leave your studying to the last week or few days before the exam. Here are some well-practised study techniques that will help you throughout the year.

1. Keep a notebook with key phrases and business terminology.
2. Make up your own PowerPoint revision presentations.
3. Draw memory maps or spider diagrams to help you remember key points.
4. Team up with a friend and get them to ask you questions.
5. Practise past exam paper questions.
6. Read quality newspapers and business websites.

7. Look after your health and wellbeing – eat a healthy diet, drink plenty of water and take regular exercise breaks.

8. On the day of the exam, you will feel proud that you have prepared and cannot criticise yourself by saying *'if only I had done more…'.*

GOOD LUCK!